FOREWORD BY BISHOP

CHANGE
Is
On
The Way
You Must Not Miss It!

JOSEPH NATHANIEL ACQUAYE

FRESH OIL
FOR
FRESH CHANGE.

[signature]
25/10/17.

FOREWORD BY BISHOP CLEMENT ASIHENE

Change

Is

On

The Way

You Must Not Miss It!

JOSEPH NATHANIEL ACQUAYE

CHANGE IS ON THE WAY

Published by: Joseph Nathaniel Acquaye

First Printed in England by: Creative Design and Print Centre,

6 The Boulevard,

Balham High Street,

London SW17 7BW

Copyright 2014 by Joseph Nathaniel Acquaye

Contact:

Mobile: +44 7868753988

Email: Joe.acquaye@yahoo.co.uk

ISBN 978-0-9930482-0-3

Unless otherwise indicated, all scripture quotations are from the King James Version of the Bible.

All Rights reserved. No Part of this publication may be reproduced, stored in a retrieval system, or transmitted, in any form or by any means, electronic, mechanical, photocopying and /or otherwise without prior written permission of the publisher.

CONTENTS

Dedication 4

endorsements 5

Acknowledgements 6

Foreword 8

Introduction 10

Background Story 13

CHAPTER 1 Agents of Change 14

CHAPTER 2 The Bait Of Accusation 19

CHAPTER 3 The Purpose of God 25

CHAPTER 4 The Faithful Messenger 36

CHAPTER 5 Time Is Ticking 43

CHAPTER 6 The Master Chemist 50

CHAPTER 7 Divine Appointment 57

CHAPTER 8 Availability not ability 63

CHAPTER 9 Get ready for a testimony 76

CHAPTER 10 Best for Last 83

CHAPTER 11 Change and your sacrifice 92

CHAPTER 12 In Whose Counsel Are You Walking? 110

CHAPTER 13 Loosed Change 129

CHAPTER 14 Total Freedom 137

CHAPTER 15 Conclusion 162

DEDICATION

I dedicate this book to my late beloved father Daniel Alotey Kwao Acquaye, affectionately called Braa Dan. I specially thank God for blessing me with such a father who did not just teach me love but also showed me love and as far as I am concerned, I could not have had a better earthly father. He thought me to be honest and forgiving. He encouraged me to be charitable and to love humanity. He taught me the Lord's Prayer in Ga (my local dialect) and to love God, a value I hold in very high esteem and graciously cherish.

Dad was so passionate about education and wanted me to have the very best no matter what it cost him. He took me through Soul Clinic International School, one of the best in Ghana, for my primary education and I am ever so grateful.

He taught me to dress as a gentleman and to live as a gentleman. He worked for Ghana Airways, the then National Airline as a Senior Interline Accountant, with great passion and commitment to duty; an observation that inspired me to do likewise wherever I am blessed to serve.

Dad was blessed with great vocals with which he served as a chorister at various Anglican Churches in Accra and also became a highlife artist. He was the writer and singer of a large percentage of highlife songs such as 'Abele' Yaa Tawo Ono, Sunday Mirror, Eyimi Eyimi' etc. under the then E.T. Mensah Tempos Band. He later had his own band 'The Planets'. He played all over Ghana as well as some parts of West Africa and also featured on GBC TV programmes such as Band Stand, Musical Rendezvous, The Mike Eghan Show and others.

Even though you are gone, the legacy you left testifies of your presence on earth. I Love you Dad, You are a LEGEND!

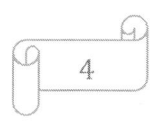

ENDORSEMENTS

An invaluable book that provides a moving and practical life account of the word of God. This book "Change Is On the Way" reveals an in-depth knowledge of the Love of God and the truth that challenges ones faith to experience change. It inspires and brings hope to hopeless situations. "An outstanding piece of work" which intends to benefit believers, non-believers and those in Ministry. This is a book to read if you desire Change.

Cynthia Sutherland
Registered Nurse, UK
Church Elder, VBCI-UK

"This is a lovely book, full of heart and wisdom. It is an offering from a true spiritual brother and friend. *'Change Is On the Way'* is an invaluable, compassionate, and spiritual harvest of great insights that will both excite and challenge the reader. This affirming message of hope and healing is a must read. Rev. Joe is a gem to be treasured". Bless you my brother...

Rev. Sammy Okae
Senior IT Auditor
Bank of Ghana

The book "Change Is On The Way" addresses a topic that will challenge today's Christian to strive for positive change. The instructions and lessons in this book will truly teach, encourage, empower and prepare anyone for the change that God will bring into their lives. This is not just a well written book, it is also well researched, well thought out and above all, based on the word of God.

Bishop Richard Aryee
Lighthouse Chapel Int. - UK

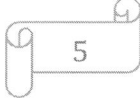

ACKNOWLEDGEMENTS

I thank God almighty, for His word which has been my main resource towards this book. I thank Him for His grace and mercies that have seen me through all challenges in the process.

Bishop N. A. Tackie-Yarboi, Presiding Bishop of VBCI worldwide, I thank God for your life Sir and for your teaching anointing that trickles down to us by God's grace.

I thank my Spiritual Father, Bishop Clement for spotting a gift and potential in me, I never saw in myself and for all the support he has provided me and my family throughout the years, especially in the birth of my ministry. I am highly indebted. Thank your Sir!

Rev. Mrs. Cecilia Asihene; Mummy, you are a blessing to us. Thank you so much.

I thank God for the life of Elder Jacob Aryee of VBCI Mercy Sanctuary, who sowed the first seed of encouragement in me to write a book. It might have been a simple encouragement at that time, but this is how far it has brought us. Nii, God bless you. You are a treasured son and friend.

Dr. Lawrence Tetteh, thank you for your inspiration, friendship and dependable support. God bless you Sir!

Rev. Samuel Senyo Okae, my good friend! Thank you for your encouragement and support in diverse ways. God bless you richly.

Mrs. Leticia Asumang, Thanks for the reading and encouragement.

Mrs. Cynthia Sutherland, you are such a blessing! Thanks for reading through, editing, your motivation and general support. God bless you.

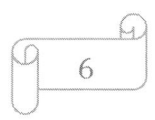

All the VBCI Midlands Pastors and congregation, I say God richly bless you for your love, relationship and prayers.

A very special mention to VBCI Mercy Sanctuary Members. I am so grateful. Your labour of Love shall be a permanent memorial before the King of kings. God bless you abundantly.

To my dear mother, Miss Dora Akweley Quaye, my sister Mrs. Gloria Okae, my brothers Pastor Richard Acquaye, Henry Acquaye, Abraham Acquaye, Mark Nii Addo Acquaye and cousin Richard Debrah, thank you all for your prayers and support.

Massive thanks to my wife, Pastor Judith Acquaye for the encouragement and constant pressure to get this book going and also for your proof reading. You are a pillar! God bless you abundantly!

Very Special thanks to my wonderful children Daniel Alotey Acquaye, Joseph Alotei Acquaye, Lennox Adokwei Acquaye, Rubi Naa Adoley Acquaye and Mrs. Shannade Acquaye, for their encouragement and excitement at this project. It's been wonderful and motivating. Thank you so much. God Bless you ever so richly.

I love you all.

FOREWORD

Between where we are and where we want to be is one word: CHANGE.

This gift has only been given to humans. Thus, if you don't like your life you can change it. Animals can't change theirs, neither can trees. Man is not a tree stuck in one place. He can move to different places if he doesn't like his environment.

No matter how far you've gone from your purpose or destiny, or messed up, you still have the power of choice to change every situation by the grace of God. Change is God's gift to people who find themselves removed or separated from their destiny, making it possible for them to bridge the gap.

People who don't change know they can do so at any time, so they keep postponing. However, if a deadline or a 'chairos' moment of opportunity is put on change, you will be amazed how quickly many will.

Change begins in OUR MINDS. It is an undramatic thing that happens in the mind because it takes you to make a decision that says 'I can't live like this anymore'. The day you decide to prosper, you will start prospering. The day you decide to walk in love and not bitterness you just decide to walk in the realm of God.

Don't let circumstances determine when to change. You take charge of your circumstances by utilising the various principles and destiny helpers outlined in this book by Rev Joe Acquaye.

Going through this book tells me that God doesn't want us to live our lives by default but by design.

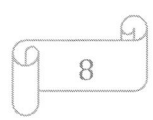

CHANGE IS ON THE WAY, could be the turning point for someone who has encountered terrible things in his or her life, and has given up or is about to give up because the price to change was too expensive. It is time to seize this moment and not to live in REGRET (The price of regret is far more expensive than that of change).

Like the man born blind in John Chapter 9, Jesus is passing, therefore seize this moment to change your destiny. Your best days are ahead of you, but your worst days are behind you.

SHALOM
Bishop Clement Asihene

(Sector Overseer, VBCI Europe & Asia)

INTRODUCTION

This book has been written to encourage the reader about the gift of change for believers and unbelievers alike. It highlights the love of God which He graciously sends to His children, surrounding them with their desired changes and resources. It raises some awareness concerning various life situations and brings out the beautiful picture of God's love for humanity which should not be missed.

It is a known fact that change is an inevitable aspect of life which everybody experiences daily. There are two types of change. We have 'Positive change' and 'Negative change'. In this book I focus more on the positive aspect of change. I would further state that positive change also comes in two dimensions. There is what I term 'Evolutionary change' and also 'Revolutionary change'. In evolutionary change the process as the name implies, is slow whereas in the revolutionary change, the process is comparatively more radical and rapid such that is almost impossible to intercept.

This book looks at some healing form of changes in scripture, starting with the story of the boy born blind in John 9:1-9. However, I wish to prepare your mind that the writing goes into a subroutine where relevant, in order to integrate and reasonably discuss further details of linkable scriptural stories to elucidate various verses of the main story and then returns, thereby bringing out appreciable lessons that make it not just 'a wanting to read' but also thought provoking.

As a young totally inexperienced pastor who started ministry with very limited scriptural knowledge, and also generally nervous, I struggled to learn and preach to a congregation some of which knew more than I did and had probably heard better sermons. As the week drew to an end and Sunday approached, I became even more nervous as to what to preach that would make positive impact in the lives of my congregation of which about 90% were first degree graduates and Master's degree holders. This book would hopefully help some pastors like me and teachers of various capacities in Church with the few revelations and extracted juices in the scriptures, thereby helping them derive sermons out of it and also make it a starting line for their own revelations, sermon development, enhancement and general knowledge that would add to the expansion, appreciation and admiration of the gospel.

Others who may be going through various forms of challenges and on the verge of quitting, may also draw some inspiration from this book, to keep on pushing forward, employing and engaging the principles that attract positive change.

Years ago, my wife enrolled at the University to pursue a degree course in Nursing. She met other matured students on the course who had been working as health care assistants in the Nursing industry and therefore, were reasonably familiar with procedures and terminologies. On the contrary, my wife had absolutely no clue to the extent that, she asked questions which happened to be too basic for someone pursuing the course to raise. She expected them to encourage her, since they were all matured and in the forty age bracket. Unfortunately, they brought her spirit rather lower with comments that made it very difficult for her to ask questions to which she needed answers and explanation, at lectures. Eventually she decided to quit the course but I stood and drew on my personal experience, which I have shared in this book to console and encourage her. As time went on, some of those who thought she had bitten more than she could chew by enrolling on the course, rather dropped out due to the momentum and intensity the course gained with time. With the primary help of God and secondary counsel from my experience, she saw her desired change come to fruition and at present she is working as a unit manager in a reputable care home.

What a difference, what a contrast? Enjoy this book and prepare for your own change, which is on the way.

BACKGROUND STORY
(John 9:1-9 NIV)

1 As he went along, he saw a man blind from birth. 2 His disciples asked him, "Rabbi, who sinned, this man or his parents, that he was born blind?"

3 "Neither this man nor his parents sinned," said Jesus, "but this happened so that the works of God might be displayed in him. 4 As long as it is day, we must do the works of him who sent me. Night is coming, when no one can work. 5 While I am in the world, I am the light of the world."

6 After saying this, he spit on the ground, made some mud with the saliva, and put it on the man's eyes. 7 "Go," he told him, "wash in the Pool of Siloam" (this word means "Sent"). So the man went and washed, and came home seeing.

8 His neighbours and those who had formerly seen him begging asked, "Isn't this the same man who used to sit and beg?" 9 Some claimed that he was. Others said, "No, he only looks like him."

But he himself insisted, "I am the man."

There are various concepts that I find very interesting and well noting from the scripture above which is in itself a follow-on from the end of the previous chapter in the Bible:

58 "Very truly I tell you," Jesus answered, "before Abraham was born, I am!" 59 At this, they picked up stones to stone him, but Jesus hid himself, slipping away from the temple grounds. John 8:58 NIV

Jesus had basically, escaped from a people who had become offended because he had said that, before Abraham was, he is. As a result of the offense they tried to stone him. Jesus hiding from the crowd, wisely slipped away in escape.

CHAPTER 1

AGENTS OF CHANGE

Every creature can be an agent of change due to the power and authority of God over us. However as Christians in particular, called of God, volunteered to be servants and examples of Christ who was not just an agent of change and healing but healing himself, there are basics that would help us keep and discharge our duties effectively as Christ did in the above scripture of the boy born blind.

NOT ALL FIGHTS ARE NECESSSARY

As an agent of healing and change in general, you must understand from the Scripture above that, there are certain fights that are not necessary and must be avoided if possible. You owe no one a demonstration of God's power in you or with you, neither should you be drawn into unnecessary combat by the devil nor his agents of distraction. The Bible says that:

"A fool shows his annoyance at once, but a prudent man overlooks an insult."-Proverbs 12:16

Now, although Jesus could have defended himself by the power that worked in him, he chose to slip away. It follows that in order to experience and serve as agents of God's healing you need to decide which fights are worth fighting and which ones are pure distractions. Which fights are godly fights and which ones are simply baits of the enemy that must be avoided. As a guide rule, any fight or contention that comes as a result of speaking the truth of God, becomes technically and spiritually a fight belonging to God and you must do your best to slip out of it, leaving judgement and vengeance to the Lord.

Fear ye not, stand still, and see the salvation of the LORD, which he will show to you today: for the Egyptians whom ye have seen today, ye shall see them again no more for ever. The LORD shall fight for you, and ye shall hold your peace.   Exodus 14:13-14 KJV

Fighting God's fight for him is not only taking power into your own hands but also derailing yourself from the plans and purposes of God. As a result, you rather end up letting down souls like the blind boy in the scripture, who could be depending on you as an agent of God's healing and deliverance and also depending on you to lead them to the Lord, in order to expose them to God's love and miracles. Jesus however, was smart! He chose to slip away and that aligned him on course for the beneficiary who had been born blind. It would be of no surprise that many believers have let down prospective evangelistic souls because they decided to demonstrate their powers and strengths unnecessarily.

PRAYER:

Pray that you will not be drawn into un-necessary fights that will derail you from the course of God for your life but as an Instrument of his love and his miracles of change.

LOVE BEYOND LIMITS

As an agent of healing your love for humanity is paramount. Therefore, you need to love beyond limits and without the fear and threats of the enemy. An agent is a representative backed by the power of the agency. So in your case and mine, the almighty God is our agency. Looking at the story leading on to the miracle in John 9, you would realise that although Jesus was on the escape or on the run (*so to speak*), he did not allow the stoning threat hanging round His neck to prevent him from exhibiting and living the unconditional love that his father had sent him to demonstrate. This reflects how important it is to know your mission! It is imperative to know why you exist. God created us all for a purpose and that is to bring glory and honour to his holy name by keeping his commandments, especially, that of love. Solomon puts it in a beautiful and simple way:

Let us hear the conclusion of the whole matter: Fear God, and keep his commandments: for this is the whole duty of man. Eccl12:13 KJV

Jesus sees the man who was living short of what God has freely given. He was living in captivity due to loss of his vision, right from birth. Jesus immediately stopped to attend to this man. Question is, why? Jesus was a person who knew his mission and was guided by his right prioritisation. Yes, you may know your mission alright, but wrong prioritisation would mess a good mission. Jesus knew what his father had sent him to do. To proclaim good news to the poor and to set the captives free; and he stuck to it. May we stick to what the father sent us to do in Jesus name!

The Bible says everywhere he went he was doing 'good'. It means that good deeds should be a normal lifestyle. As Christians we need to set our priorities right. First to God and His purpose for us on earth and then what we reasonable deserve, would also follow!

The need for prioritisation cannot be overemphasised in being an agent of God's healing and in fact, change in general. Jesus did not neglect this vital component of his success in life. The moment you misplace your priority, you get drawn away and out of your line of purpose and even destiny. A typical scenario can be drawn from the story of David and his own brother Eliab. The Bible says:

²⁸ When Eliab, David's oldest brother, heard him speaking with the men, he burned with anger at him and asked, "Why have you come down here? And with whom did you leave those few sheep in the wilderness? I know how conceited you are and how wicked your heart is; you came down only to watch the battle." ²⁹ "Now what have I done?" said David. "Can't I even speak?" ³⁰ He then turned away to someone else and brought up the same matter, and the men answered him as before. 1 Sam 17:28-30 NIV

In the above scripture David was almost drawn into an unnecessary quarrel by his own elder brother. However he turned away to someone else and asked him the same question. The difference was that, David did not allow himself to be drawn into a fight of sibling rivalry. His focus and priority was on silencing Goliath and that kept him on course to honour and destiny fulfilment. Likewise, may you overcome distractions and may you fulfil your destiny in Jesus name!

The Israelites including Saul himself were bewildered with fear and they needed healing out of their fear. God presented an agent of change for healing in the package of David.

Fear thou not; for I am with thee: be not dismayed; for I am thy God: I will strengthen thee; yea, I will help thee; yea, I will uphold thee with the right hand of my righteousness.
Isaiah 41:10 KJV

Had David made an attempt to fight Eliab, it could have resulted in two fundamental mistakes. One, he could have lost the lifetime opportunity of facing Goliath which could have derailed him from his allotted destiny, if not delayed it. Two, he could have probably run out of the needed strength to fight Goliath, who was the real enemy. Unfortunately, this has been a mistake among believers in many cases. Sometimes we use up all our strengths, focus and concentration in fighting each other, leaving Satan our real enemy, free. Lord help us.

It is important to spot the enemy behind various forms of distractions. In David's case for example, the enemy tried to use his own brother as distraction whiles in Jesus's case it was his own disciples, trying to divert his attention from solution orientation to unnecessary troubleshooting and route cause analysis.

Jesus said in Matthew 10:36, 'A man's foes shall be they of his own household'.

It is imperative that we know and keep our purpose, hold our priorities high and also do well everywhere we go for then we are being salt of the earth and light of the world. Salt makes better, not worse and light makes clearer not dimer. It follows that we must become difference makers just like Jesus who saw an opportunity to make a difference in the life of the boy born blind and he did not let that opportunity slip away, despite the threat of being stoned. He was ready to love beyond limits and threats, even unto death! Praise God!

***Greater love has no one than this: to lay down one's life for one's friends.** – John 15:13 NIV*

CHAPTER 2

THE BAIT OF ACCUSATION

"Rabbi, who sinned, this man or his parents, that he was born blind?"

Much as God is interested in the change and healing of His sons and daughters, the enemy is also interested in keeping the children of God in bondage through various means of sicknesses and oppressions. One of the very strategic and unfortunately effective method he uses is through the bait of accusation. In our main story we see how Jesus, an agent of healing and change was moved with compassion to the boy born blind, but the enemy had to throw in the bait of accusation in an attempt to distract Jesus and probably to justify by the law, why the boy had been born blind and therefore deserved to remain so. Watch out for the bait of accusation.

You may not be able to choose who levies accusation at you but you can choose not to be a Levite of accusation.

The Focus of Man and the Focus of God

As agents of healing and change in general, we must be mindful of God's desire and interest. The Bible says His disciples asked 'master who sinned, was it the man or His parents'. Jesus responded by saying, neither but rather, he was in that condition in order for the glory of God to be manifested.

Now, the Disciples were looking for an opportunity to point fingers and a reason to accuse but Jesus on the contrary was focusing on a reason to excuse and emancipate the boy from what would by the law, had been a wage of sin. That is why He came! To be a gift of God unto eternal life. Amen.

For the wages of sin is death, but the gift of God Is eternal life in Christ Jesus our Lord – Rom 6:23 NIV.

It is important to note that, the people who were interested in who sinned, were not new converts or just recently born-again as our present time would apply. They were actually disciples! It means that, they had followed the teachings of Christ and had more or less become duplicates of Christ, in terms of knowledge and probably disciplines. Hence, their description as disciples! However, they were rather short of the speed to demonstrate the love of God, which Christ had been demonstrating as they went along with him.

The truth and practicality of the matter is that, in our Churches today, we have a lot of 'disciples'. Disciples who are more interested in pointing fingers of accusation and highlighting the sins of others but rather missing the opportunity to show God's love and to minister the sufficient and saving grace of God!

What do we learn here? In any unfortunate situation, we need to look out for the glory of God birthing out of it as a message of His love and desire to have more people experience His grace through our saviour Jesus Christ. John 10:10, comforts us that the thief (devil) comes to steal, kill and to destroy but Jesus came so that we would have life and have it more abundantly. I think that is powerful.

Man focuses on reasons to accuse but God focuses on reasons to excuse. As a matter of fact God is more interested in being a righteousness detective than a sin detective. By the death and resurrection of Christ, God excused us from all our sins. All not just one, ALL! He focuses on the reason of the cross and hearkens to the voice and speech of our saviour's blood. What a loving God!

The Issue of Hypocrisy

God excuses us from the accusation of men, for many reasons, one of which is the mere Hypocrisy of Man. There's the possibility that, even the disciples who were asking with keen interest as to who sinned, were not perfect themselves. Their mere walk with Jesus was no certification of their righteousness or perfection.

The woman caught in the act of adultery (John 8:4) was excused and not condemned of her sin because her accusers themselves were not any better. They were not sinless. Whiles they were focusing on stoning the woman in her bondage, again, Christ on the contrary was focusing on setting her free from the same bondage and admonishing her not to sin any more. What a difference?!

John 8:1-11NIV:

¹ but Jesus went to the Mount of Olives. ² At dawn he appeared again in the temple courts, where all the people gathered around him, and he sat down to teach them. ³ The teachers of the law and the Pharisees brought in a woman caught in adultery. They made her stand before the group ⁴ and said to Jesus, "Teacher, this woman was caught in the act of adultery. ⁵ In the Law Moses commanded us to stone such women. Now what do you say?" ⁶ They were using this question as a trap, in order to have a <u>basis for accusing</u> him.

But Jesus bent down and started to write on the ground with his finger. ⁷ When they kept on questioning him, he straightened up and said to them, "Let any one of you who is without sin be the first to throw a stone at her." ⁸ Again he stooped down and wrote on the ground.

⁹ At this, those who heard began to go away one at a time, the older ones first, until only Jesus was left, with the woman still standing there. ¹⁰ Jesus straightened up and asked her, "Woman, where are they? Has no one condemned you?" ¹¹ "No one, sir," she said. "Then neither do I condemn you," Jesus declared. "Go now and leave your life of sin."

Isn't it amazing how we see the bait of accusation back in action even against Jesus in the verse 6 underlined above?

We need to point people to the cross and admonish them not to sin anymore, because a price, has already been paid for our freedom!

Whiles they, the Pharisees were trying to bury her by the law and under the law, Christ on the contrary was raising her out of the adulterous and sinful grave.

No wonder Jesus refers to Hypocrisy as the yeast of the Pharisees in Luke 12:1 NIV!

As you read this book, may the Spirit that raised Christ from the dead, raise you up and out of every form of grave in which men, society and this world at large might have tried to bury you. As Christ rose from the grave so have you risen, in Jesus name!

It is rather sad to sometimes see Christians more interested in who is sinning and who has sinned rather than who is preaching, who is teaching and who is actually witnessing and winning lost souls for Christ. In certain situations congregation have put even church leaders under intensive microscopic scrutiny to the extent that, they have misplaced and diverted their own focus from the word rather to a witch hunt, consequently, missing the opportunity to be used as miraculous instruments of God.

In the story above of the woman caught in the act of adultery, when Jesus asked that the one who has never sinned before should cast the first stone, the hypocrisy of all her accusers came to bear. May God expose all your accusers too in Jesus name!

The issue of Hypocrisy poses such an obstacle to healing ministration and reception of healing that, I think it would be reasonably useful for me to share a little bit more about its' effects.

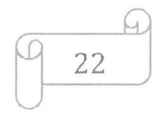

Effects of Hypocrisy

Firstly, hypocrisy can put the hypocrite to shame. Can you imagine the shameful countenance of the Pharisees as they read what Jesus was writing on the floor, believed to be the Ten Commandments and realising that, they were not without sin themselves?

Similarly, the Hypocrisy of Judah against Tamar brought shame to him whiles it relieved Tamar of the intended punishment that had been prescribed for her. See the story below:

22 And he returned to Judah, and said, I cannot find her; and also the men of the place said, that there was no harlot in this place. 23 And Judah said, Let her take it to her, lest we be shamed: behold, I sent this kid, and thou hast not found her. 24 And it came to pass about three months after, that it was told Judah, saying, Tamar thy daughter in law hath played the harlot; and also, behold, she is with child by whoredom. <u>And Judah said, bring her forth, and let her be burnt.</u> 25 When she was brought forth, she sent to her father in law, saying, By the man, whose these are, am I with child: and she said, Discern, I pray thee, whose are these, the signet, and bracelets, and staff. 26 And Judah acknowledged them, and said, She hath been more righteous than I; because that I gave her not to Shelah my son. And he knew her again no more.

Isn't it typical, how Judah was bold in asking for Tamar to be brought and burnt? One could easily have said, 'this man is without sin and very disciplined'! It's rather unfortunate how many of us as believers tend to play holier-than-thou and accuse and judge others. Lord have mercy!

Also a person's hypocrisy can unfortunately empower people who should honour and respect him to rather disrespect him with boldness. In Galatians 2:11-14 for example, Peter probably the oldest among the apostles was rebuked openly by Paul, a younger apostle, for hypocritically pretending that he had not been eating with the gentiles as a Jew. Can you imagine? I am talking about Peter; the one who caught the revelation that Jesus was Christ son of the living God! It means that the spirit of hypocrisy has no regard for age and experience neither does it recognise how much and how deep revelations you have had in the past. As much as possible we need to avoid hypocrisy and be ourselves. Our yeah should be yeah and Nay, nay. Integrity is strength!

Hypocrisy should never be underestimated. It can cause even leaders to go astray. So a hypocrite is a dangerous personality. The Bible tells us about Barnabas going astray in Gal: 2:13 due to the hypocrisy of Peter alongside some of the other Jews.

Most dangerously, Hypocrisy shuts the door to the Kingdom of Heaven. Wow!

"But woe to you, scribes and Pharisees, hypocrites! You lock up the kingdom of heaven from people. For you don't go in, and you don't allow those entering to go in. "Woe to you, scribes and Pharisees, hypocrites! You devour widows' houses and make long prayers just for show. This is why you will receive a harsher punishment. Matt 23:13-14 HCSB

From the scripture above, the state of hypocrisy is a situation requiring healing and even deliverance.

Lord heal and deliver us from the oppression of hypocrisy. Help us escape and overcome the bait of accusation and not to become accusers ourselves! Amen.

CHAPTER 3

THE PURPOSE OF GOD

"But this happened so that the works of God might be displayed in him'

Jesus the agent of healing and change explains the reason behind the boy's condition. Everybody and for that matter, every change agent has a gift and every gift, has two purposes. We all have a gift first of all for a divine personal purpose and also for a divine corporate purpose.

It must be noted that, just as God did not make man to live in isolation, so did he not give man purposes to be kept or manifested in silos but rather inter-woven into other people's purposes, for an overall demonstration of his beauty and glory.

A gift is a difference maker

Every purpose God gives to us personally, feeds into His corporate purpose in order to project a bigger picture of God's glory in the midst of His people.

Now, every gift needs an environment or circumstance in order to announce and demonstrate its purpose. Although hard, it's still fair to say that, the boy born blind's condition was an environment for the gift in Christ to demonstrate its' purpose.

The Bible says that *'A man's gift makes room for him, and brings him before great men. Prov.18:16 KJV*

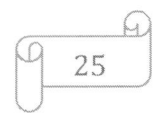

So a man's gift has a purpose and incidentally, an environment. The purpose is making room whiles the environment is 'before great men'. I must state that the greatness of a man is not based on outward appearance, physical structure, academic qualification, physical location or even social position. So the expression, *'great men'* is not necessarily measured in terms of appearance. It is actually based on the treasure God has in-built within the person which unfortunately is not visible to the naked eye and for that reason, many gifted men tend to miss the door or environment where their gift would have made the intended impact and fulfilled its purpose for them. They come before great men yet not recognising them as great and for that reason, reserve to share what God has freely given to them for the profit of all. They judge by appearance.

Judging content by a container can be erroneous and very regrettable!

It becomes easier to identify your great men when you know your gift. Jesus knew his gift and the gift led him to the great man, the blind boy. When your gift meets its appropriate soil it is impossible to overlook or bypass it. So a gift is a seed, be it within or without and when the seed meets its appropriate soil, the value within it becomes easily evident. Furthermore, no soil fights or rejects a good seed.

Don't Miss Your Great Men

The most regrettable mistake any gifted person can make is missing the great men before whom their gift would make room for them. Similarly, the sad mistake an agent of change and healing could make is to miss his beneficiaries for whom God has specially packaged and assigned to him. Every agent of healing has a God prepared reward of surprise for a faithful service.

Joseph had a gift of dream interpretation. He was an agent of healing to two depressed prisoners.

⁶ When Joseph came to them in the morning and looked at them, he saw that they were sad and <u>depressed</u>. Gen 40:6 Amplified

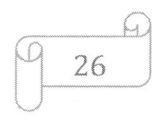

Depression is not healthy and any unhealthy situation is in need of healing.

I have written and as you read, let's jointly declare and decree total healing out of every form of depression plaguing our loved ones in Jesus name! Amen

The environment Joseph needed to use his gift for elevation or promotion was not in the house of Potiphar, who was captain of Pharaoh's palace, but rather, a fellow prisoner; ordinary and common like any of the other prisoners he had with him. The difference was that Joseph had an in-built purpose of treasure as against any of his fellow prisoners. Given an opportunity to guess or rate between the two environments, many of us would have rated Potiphar's house as an environment more likely to lead to elevation, over the Prison and the prisoner. Thank God Joseph did not allow the social status of people to determine whom he would share his gift with or serve his gift to. The Cupbearer was a great man and the prison could not annul that. He was carrying an in-built treasure of God and was therefore a fertile soil or opportunity for Joseph. When you carry an in-built treasure of God, it cannot be suppressed by any form of darkness nor misfortune, it will certainly shine through! There may be people in rather unfortunate and even disgraceful situations but could still be the great men you need. Whiles you read this book as a gifted man or woman, an agent of God's healing and change in general, I pray that you will not miss your great men.

Let Your Best Be Your Standard

It is very easy to miss your great men before whom your gift could make the necessary impact. At the same time it is very easy to gain and seize such opportunities. The success secret is **'let your best, be your standard'**. In other words, don't decide on or discriminate as to where and when and to whom you would give and share your best. Whatever you do, do it as unto the Lord! If you can use your gift bearing in mind the omnipresence of God, your best will always be your standard and there's no way you will miss your great men! If you don't miss your great men, you would not miss your reward. You have a great reward, so don't miss it. Change is on the way !

God Is No Respecter of Persons

Both agents and beneficiaries of change have great destinies and as a child of God, you are not exempted. However, it's important to bear in mind that, every person of destiny has what I call 'destiny facilitators'. Now, although nobody needs everybody, everybody needs somebody and for that simple reason, God can use anybody as your destiny facilitator. God works based on who or what is available rather than who qualifies. A donkey is not qualified to counsel a man but when the need became imperative God caused a donkey to counsel and even rebuke a man:

Then the LORD opened the donkey's mouth, and she asked Balaam, "What have I done to you that you have beaten me these three times?" - Numbers 22:28 HCSB

There's a beautiful illustration I love concerning David in scripture to which I would like to divert in order to elucidate this even more:

[14] Now the Spirit of the LORD had departed from Saul, and an evil spirit from the LORD tormented him.

[15] Saul's attendants said to him, "See, an evil spirit from God is tormenting you. [16] Let our lord command his servants here to search for someone who can play the harp. He will play when the evil spirit from God comes upon you, and you will feel better."

17 So Saul said to his attendants, "Find someone who plays well and bring him to me."

18 <u>One of the servants</u> answered, "<u>I have seen</u> a son of Jesse of Bethlehem who knows how to play the harp. He is a brave man and a warrior. <u>He speaks well </u>and is a fine-looking man. <u>And the LORD is with him</u>." *19* Then Saul sent messengers to Jesse and said, "Send me your son David, who is with the sheep." *20* So Jesse took a donkey loaded with bread, a skin of wine and a young goat and sent them with his son David to Saul.

21 David came to Saul and entered his service. Saul liked him very much, and David became one of his armor-bearers. *22* Then Saul sent word to Jesse, saying, "Allow David to remain in my service, for I am pleased with him."

23 Whenever the spirit from God came upon Saul, David would take his harp and play. Then relief would come to Saul; he would feel better, and the evil spirit would leave him. 1 Samuel 16:14-23. NIV

We see from the above scripture that when Saul, needed healing and deliverance from the torment of an evil spirit and as such was looking for someone (agent of healing) to play the harp for the evil spirit that tormented him to depart, it was one of his servants that recommended David. It was not another king anywhere. It was a servant! It was the servant that facilitated that destiny of David. He said 'I have seen a son of Jesse, he is a warrior and plays the harp'. It is worth bearing in mind that, it was the servant who had seen David and not necessarily the other way round. It cannot be over emphasised that it is imperative to be at and do your best at all times, because you never know who may be watching you and who your future referee could be.

Everybody has a referee or an advertiser; someone to introduce and announce you. John the Baptist for example, was the referee and announcer of Jesus Christ whiles the cupbearer was the advertiser of

Joseph to Pharaoh. You never know who yours is and where he or she might see you. You cannot afford to disappoint your advertiser. You must be impressive and at your best at all times even in the remotest of environments. Your advertiser and referee to the King could be observing you with a sincere, keen and un-distractible interest.

There is an adage that goes like *'it's whom you know'*; which simply means that, to breakthrough in life, you must know someone of influence. However I have formed a different opinion and that is what I recommend living by. That, it's not a matter of *whom you know*, but rather *who knows you*? I have come across a number of people who claim to know someone of a prominent and celebrity status, when as a matter of fact the celebrity has no knowledge of them at all.

Speak Well

The servant among other accolades about David, mentions that, he speaks well and is fine looking. Everybody is blessed with good looks by dint of being in the image and likeness of God. However, the skill of politeness and well speaking is a personal responsibility which must be taken and also mastered because apart from other benefits, it attracts unprecedented blessings of change from God and when God himself has blessed you, who can curse you?

You are the most handsome of men; grace flows from your lips. Therefore God has blessed you forever Psalm 45:2 HCSB

The word '*Therefore*' in the above scripture says it all. That, even your way and good manner of speaking stands to attract blessing. So in addition to being a gifted person and in this case, an agent and also a beneficiary of change, you need to be gracious in speech. No wonder Bible admonishes us to let our speech be seasoned with salt.

Let your speech be always with grace, seasoned with salt, that ye may know how ye ought to answer every man. Col 4:6 KJV

It's so amazing the difference 'well speaking' can make in a person's life. I am not talking so much of eloquence, but prudence. Two criminals were hanged with Jesus. One of them gained an entry into Paradise simply by the prudence in his speech (Luke 23:42-43) whiles the other missed that opportunity due to the opposite.

He positioned himself for total damnation by speaking to make mockery of Jesus.

The eye that mocketh at his father, and despiseth to obey his mother, the ravens of the valley shall pick it out, and the young eagles shall eat it. Proverbs 30:17 KJV

Could it be possible that there are some that are living with their physical sight intact but their spiritual eyes or visionary eyes have been picked out and for that reason though surrounded by opportunities of gold, they cannot see? It is a serious thing to mock 'a father' be it spiritual or biological. Always speak well of your father, it's better to be silent on their short-falls than to publicise it in ridicule because there is no blessing in it whatsoever!

The Lord with Him

Another accolade about David the servant highlighted was the fact that the Lord was with him. Every agent of change and healing needs the company of the Lord's presence, which is basically the Holy Spirit. It follows that as agents of healing and change in general just like David, we should crave for the Lord's presence as if our life depends solely on it.

Cast me not away from thy presence; and take not thy holy spirit from me. Psalm 51:11 KJV

It is very possible to be in the Lord's presence without the presence of the Lord necessarily being with you and this is something David appreciated in the above scripture.

Jesus Christ gives us a hint of formulae that can retain God's presence with you, which is to aim at doing what pleases God always:

The One who sent Me is with Me. He has not left Me alone, <u>because</u> I always do what pleases Him." John 8:29 HSCB

Divine Purposes

Now back to continue on gifts and purposes, Joseph had a personal purpose given by God, which is what I refer to as divine personal purpose and that was for Joseph to rise to prominence as prime minister although a foreigner, which further confirms that God is no respecter of persons. However, the corporate purpose was for the physical salvation and deliverance of the Jews out of the threat of famine and Joseph was the agent God used to bring about that change and deliverance.

*But as for you, you thought evil against me; but God meant it unto good, to bring to pass, as it is this day, **to save many people alive**. Gen. 50:20 KJV*

Purpose Unveiled Out of Obscurity

When God is working His purpose through His agents, mostly it is not easy to identify from the on-set. This is because the purposes are mostly unveiled out of Obscurity and difficulty. Joseph for example had a purpose but it was unveiled in a rather obscured place which was the Prison. You could be an agent of healing and change in general, marked for the top. However, it is very easy to lose hope, when you find yourself in a situation you never expected to be a part of that journey to the top, because many a time, they bear no resemblance whatsoever to what you see as the picture of your destiny. Now, if the place of obscurity is where your destiny facilitators are located or even bound, that would be your best place of visit or positioning.

Sometimes your best place would look like a breakers yard; messy and scrappy but also required for forging ahead! It is your break forth point. Your break forth point can sometimes look like your breakdown point but that is where you actually have to rest and trust God even more!

As a matter of fact every single day of your disappointment is also a day closer to your appointment, so keep strong and keep trusting the God who knows the thought He has towards you. Thoughts of good and not of evil. Thoughts that would bring you to His expected end. In the story of Joseph, the cisterns and prisons looked like detours and off-tracks to his destiny and divine destination but in reality, they were divinely marked stations and short-cuts to the palace of Pharaoh which his brothers, Potiphar and his wife mistakenly employed. In similar situations, God will turn every evil intention of your enemies into your favourable attention!

Joseph's personal purpose of rising to Prime Minister was a feeder into God's corporate purpose of saving the Jews from starvation, due to the famine of the day, in that region.

As could be read from the book of Judges, Gideon's purpose was likewise unveiled in a winepress. Very obscure and with absolutely no resemblance whatsoever to a battlefield where mighty men of valour are recognised and celebrated but that was where his purpose was actually unveiled. The Bible says:

The angel of the LORD came and sat down under the oak in Ophrah that belonged to Joash the Abiezrite, where his son Gideon was threshing wheat in a winepress to keep it from the Midianites - Judges 6:11 NIV

Gideon was probably on the verge of breaking down. He was doing a right thing but rather in a wrong environment, a process which more than likely, yielded very limited results. He had almost lost the confidence that God was with him as per Judges 6:13.

His purpose was unveiled out of obscurity. He rose to fulfil his personal God given purpose as a Judge in Israel, though from the least clan in the smallest tribe. Probably like Gideon you are also from a very humble background and even in a very obscure circumstance but your light and purpose is about to break forth, in Jesus name! Change is definitely on the way!

The Esther Purpose

Esther similarly had a purpose and was an agent of deliverance but was in obscurity, in the form of an exile. Her purpose was not even known to herself and it took her cousin Mordecai to hint her of her purpose. It's obviously very important to spot your co-agents or divine mentors who God brings your way to keep you on course:

[14] For if you remain silent at this time, relief and deliverance for the Jews will arise from another place, but you and your father's family will perish. And who knows but that you have come to your royal position for such a time as this?"   Esther 4:14 NIV.

Always remember that as a child of God you have a personal purpose and no matter what, as long as you are connected to the Lord, that purpose will be unveiled and displayed openly in His corporate purpose.

"Remain in me, as I also remain in you. No branch can bear fruit by itself; it must remain in the vine. Neither can you bear fruit unless you

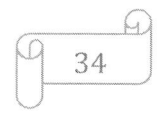

remain in me. I am the vine; you are the branches. If you remain in me and I in you, you will bear much fruit; apart from me you can do nothing. -John 15:4-5.

From the above scripture remaining in Christ and connecting to him enables you to bear much *fruit*. It is important to note the word 'fruit', as to vegetables. Fruits have seeds that enable a replica reproduction but vegetables have no seeds therefore reproduction may only be similar but not replica. In order to fulfil your God-given purpose generationally, you must remain generationally connected to Christ.

So in the story about the boy born blind for example, Jesus knew His purpose and therefore employed all the necessary skills and qualities of an agent of healing and change.

As an agent of change and healing, may you know your purpose and apply all the necessary skills and qualities that we have learnt and of course anymore that the Lord reveals to you. Amen.

CHAPTER 4

THE FAITHFUL MESSENGER
(As long as it is day, we must do the works of him who sent me.)

A messenger is a person who carries a message or goes on an errand for another, especially as a matter of duty or business. So a faithful messenger is the person who discharges this duty with passionate commitment and loyalty to the master on whose behalf the message or service is delivered or rendered respectively.

Jesus mentions in the above verse of John 9, that we must do the works of His father who sent him. Is it not refreshing and encouraging to note the team playing statement of Jesus? He has made himself a partner to the task. He said '**we must** do the **works** *of Him who sent me.* Jesus valued teamwork. From His statement, we can safely deduce that He was the one who was sent by His father but he recognised the value of more hands on deck for the harvest is always plentiful but it's the labourers that are unfortunately few. We must! It means that there's no option and no ambiguity. There is no room for excuses, because God Himself has given to us all we need to fulfil His plans and purposes here on this earth. Praise God!

Also, He did not say work, but *works.* It means, not just one thing or one of the things but everything that the sender would do in similar circumstances, we are to replicate it as representatives. It follows that we must have the spirit of the sender. That is the duty and expectation of a faithful messenger; an ambassador.

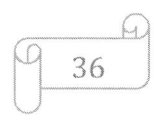

Who is an ambassador? An "ambassador" is one who "has been given the power and authority to speak and act on behalf of the kingdom he represents. He is a diplomatic minister of the highest rank, accredited as permanent representative to another country or sovereign; he is sent on a special mission, one of the first rank with treaty-signing powers." So for the Christian that means that you and I have been given power and authority to speak and act on behalf of the King of the Kingdom of Heaven, here on earth and it's when we do this faithfully, that the master who has called and empowered us is refreshed.

As the cold of snow in the time of harvest, so is a faithful messenger to them that send him: for he refresheth the soul of his masters.
Prov. 25:13 KJV

The time of harvest is a summer period or a hot season. As such the process of harvesting causes the harvesters to get tired quicker and become desperate for water and due to the probable sweat, they become desperate for cold water or ice. When they receive the water or ice, it refreshes and reenergises them to go on harvesting with renewed strength. This is the imagery effect on God when he finds faithful messengers. He is energised to do more for us. Do more to see good news land in the laps of the poor and needy. Exactly what Jesus sought to do; to refresh the father! He says:

For I came down from heaven, not to do mine own will, but the will of him that sent me. John 6:38 KJV

As a faithful messenger of God, you need to keep a yardstick as to whether or not you are refreshing the Father. When you refresh the father, He would in turn refresh you with coastal expansion and territorial increase. Remember that your refreshment of the master is a seed and therefore has a time of bountiful refreshment harvest. Harvest is always more and in multiple fold.

In the parable of the talents, it was those who did as the master expected and appreciated that got more talents and likewise the parable of the minas, '*take charge of 10 cities*'.

It is the will and desire of God that we live in prosperity and be in good health even as our souls prosper (3 John 1). It follows that God will do anything to see His children prosper spiritually and even financially.

He brought them forth also with silver and gold: and there was not one feeble person among their tribes. Psalm 105:37 KJV

Just as God brought the Israelites out of Egypt, not just with silver and gold, which is money, he also ensured that none of them was feeble. When a person is financially unwell, he or she needs money and when a person is physically or biologically unwell, they need better health. Similarly, God wants you to be healthy in every shape and every form and he would use any available person or persons to represent him and act as an extension of his hand in your circumstance, so healing is on the way, healing is here! Don't miss it.

Jesus said I must do the works of Him who sent me. I must drop all my personal objectives and preferences to do what my sender will have me do! Wow, that is powerful. God is at work and your change no matter what is within your grasp.

A faithful messenger sees joy even in the pain of serving the Lord. In Mark 15:21, bible records that on the way to crucifixion, a certain man from Cyrene called Simon who was passing by on his way from the country, was forced by the Roman soldiers to carry the cross of Jesus.

A certain man from Cyrene, Simon, the father of Alexander and Rufus, was passing by on his way in from the country, and they forced him to carry the cross. Mark 15:21 NIV

The fact that he was from Cyrene a Greek city, technically and politically makes him a Greek rather than a Jew. This reminds me of the Good Samaritan and also the foreign leper who happened to be the only one out of the healed ten that came to give thanks to Jesus in Luke 17. They were both foreigners who did what would have been expected more of the Jews in those circumstances. They were more faithful to the message of Christ than Jesus's own people. This throws a challenge to us as Christians to live to the Lord's expectation rather than neglecting and relegating our duties to unbelievers.

The Bible makes it clear that he was forced. This means he did not volunteer, however he seemed to have complied faithfully. I can only imagine how this act would have refreshed Jesus and indeed God the father himself. For once and for a change, somebody was carrying something for Jesus and sharing his burden. What a spiritual investment?! As a result of this, Simon has now become a biblical celebrity. If he is not remembered at all, at least Every Easter he would be remembered along with Jesus. May you also encounter a change to make you a celebrity in the faith! In this day and age, when a person becomes a celebrity, it brings about a great change; spiritually, financially, socially and even generationally and yours is on the way today, in Jesus name!

As Simon was forcefully drafted into the Lord's service, the nation of Cyrene was placed on the Biblical map for the first time in the gospel account of Matthew. It means that there is a tendency to raise the profile of our countries and nations and of course our churches just by serving the Lord and being faithful messengers.

As the scriptures indicate, Simon was passing by. Probably minding his own business quietly, but the enemies of the Lord forced him into carrying the cross; a situation that they thought would degrade and humiliate him rather propelled him into the limelight, making him an honourable and remarkable person in life. A reflection of Joseph and his brothers who meant evil for him, but God meant it for good. Like Joseph, Simon was accelerated into his destiny of change and purpose. We can verify from scripture that, after this scenario, Simon of Cyrene was not explicitly mentioned in scripture again. What a fulfilment of destiny!

Simon was accidentally forced into covenant with Jesus as a result of the cross he was made to carry. This is because the soldiers did not realise the spiritual imposition they were placing upon Simon and the dramatic change in the life of Simon they were effecting. What a favourable accident! Why do I say that? As a Greek, he had nothing to do with Jews who looked down upon them, as Greeks.

The woman was a Greek, a Syrophenician by nation; and she besought him that he would cast forth the devil out of her daughter. "First let the children eat all they want," he told her, "for it is not right to take the children's bread and toss it to the dogs." Mark 7:26-27 KJV

No wonder he had to be forced out of his likely reluctant and defensive demeanour.

Now though he was forced, the fact still remains that he did it. You may recall from scripture that, one day Jesus gave a parable about 2 sons (Matthew 21:28-32). In the Parable, Jesus told a story and drew a contrast between a son who said he would work but did not, and another son who said he would not but then repented and did his father's wishes. It is understood that the former son was a representation of the leadership of Israel who agreed to the covenant but rejected it. Whiles latter son represented the publicans and prostitutes whose lives were sinful but were willing to repent. This part of the repentant heart is where I would like to place Simon the Cyrene, forced to carry the cross and effectively entering into covenant with Jesus. Furthermore, by carrying the cross of Jesus, Simon was automatically sharing in Jesus's suffering. Oh Glory!

I would further deduce that, since Jesus was bleeding, the cross would have been soiled with the blood. Therefore by Simon carrying the cross of the bleeding Jesus, he would have more likely than not, brought himself into direct contact with the precious and purifying blood of Jesus. No wonder he became an instantly transformed man by the end of his service and assistance to Jesus.

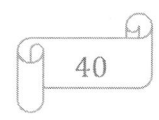

Now, though outside scripture, when you consider what has been termed and marked places as 'Stations of the Cross', there are fourteen of them. The fifth station is the point or place (*In Jerusalem, this is the location on the corner where the Via Dolorosa turns west off al-Wad Road and begins to narrow as it goes uphill.*) at which Simon of Cyrene carried the Cross, and since five happens to be the number of grace, I see it as no mere coincidence. God was definitely at work.

The grace of God located Simon at that very point of his spiritual need of change, the glory of God fell on him and everything about him changed. May that be your story too in Jesus name!

Just as aprons and handkerchiefs that had touched Apostle Paul's body were healing and changing the circumstance of people due to the anointing in them, so would the cross of Christ have impacted Simon of Cyrene even more. May the blood of Jesus speed up your change too and may the glory of the Lord rise upon you and May you shine in Jesus name!

A generational result and impact emerged from carrying the cross. Simon's sons Alexander and Rufus are mentioned with dignity for their father's sake and also for the role Rufus in particular, subsequently played in spreading the gospel of Jesus Christ.

Greet Rufus, the one chosen by the Lord, and his mother, who has been a mother to me, too – Rom 16:13 NIV

Rufus is described by Paul as 'the one chosen by the Lord'. This reminds me of Bezalel:

Then the L*ord* *said to Moses,* *² "See, I have chosen Bezalel son of Uri, the son of Hur, of the tribe of Judah,* *³ and I have filled him with the Spirit of God, with wisdom, with understanding, with knowledge and with all kinds of skills—* *⁴ to make artistic designs for work in gold, silver and bronze,* *⁵ to cut and set stones, to work in wood, and to engage in all kinds of crafts.* Exo 31:1-5 NIV

In the above scripture we realise how the connection of Bezalel to Hur is highlighted. Hur was the man who in partnership with Aaron held and kept Moses's hand up, when they came out of the wilderness to the valley of Rephidim and defeated the Amalekites through the sustained prayer hands of Moses.

The glory that came upon Bazelel could be linked to the faithful service of Hur, his grandfather and likewise the grace of God that fell upon Rufus, son of Simon of Cyrene, a faithful messenger! Now, what I wish to share with you here is that, once the master is refreshed by our faithful service, our reward will surely come. I wish to encourage that, a faithful messenger will not always reap and enjoy the rewards directly but it could go on straight to his or her descendants. Why do I say that?

Hur lifted Moses's hand but there is no recording of any reward directly for him nor Uri his son, but rather his grandson Bazelel. Sometimes God reserves the rewards to our faithful service for our descendants who might be in a better capacity and dispensation to make a better effect of the blessing and reward. Your reward to bring about an indelible and generational change is in being a faithful messenger of Jesus.

"As long as the earth endures, seedtime and harvest, cold and heat, summer and winter, day and night will never cease." Gen 8:22 NIV

The bible also mentions the mother of Rufus, being just like a mother to Paul. It follows that Simon being a selfless faithful messenger ignited a great revival in his family to include his wife to such an extent that, she was supportive of Paul's ministry. We can clearly appreciate the effect of Simon's service to our Lord Jesus in His painful hours upon his entire family. What a harvest of refreshment!

CHAPTER 5

TIME IS TICKING

Night is coming, when no one can work.

In the story of the boy born blind, Jesus was very conscious of time. It is important to bear in mind that time is constantly progressive and cannot be redeemed nor stagnated except by divine intervention. God was extremely gracious in the time and instance of Joshua.

So the sun stood still, and the moon stopped, till the nation avenged itself on its enemies, as it is written in the Book of Jashar. The sun stopped in the middle of the sky and delayed going down about a full day. Joshua 10:13

Time is not like a game. It is not like a football championship final which is designed to go into an extra time and even unto penalty shoot-outs when the allotted time to find a winner runs out. No.

As a matter of fact, everybody had a pre-paid deposit time account probably before we were conceived. This is because some of our ordinations were prior to conception. God told Jeremiah 'Before I formed you in the womb I knew you; and before you came forth out of the womb I sanctified you, and I ordained you a prophet unto the nations. (Jeremiah 1:5) and King David confirms this in Psalm 139:16:

"Your eyes saw my unformed body; all the days ordained for me were written in your book before one of them came to be." Psalm139:16 NIV

Of all that God has graciously entrusted to us to manage, our time is possibly our most precious possession. What makes our time even more essential is the fact that from the very first day we were born, it began ticking and actually, running out. Unlike our bank or investment accounts, none of us knows the balance in our time account neither do we have a means of checking it like we are able to do of our bank balances. We only know that every single day that passes and in fact every hour that passes by, it is lessening. It is often said that the moment we are born, we start dying. Now, furthermore, unlike our financial accounts into which we could make additional and periodic deposits and consequently build the account up further for the future, you cannot make any additional deposits into your time account. The best you could probably do is to work overtime and ahead of schedule, but the question is who actually determines and assesses whether or not you are indeed ahead of schedule, in the unknown future? Moreover, working overtime is not a means of redeeming any lost time but actually a means of eating into another time of a future event. No wonder, Moses wisely prays to God, the one in charge, the one who knows, saying:

So teach us to number our days, that we may apply our hearts unto wisdom. Psalm 90:12 KJV.

The understanding and appreciation of this fact would help in the disciplined approach to life and victory over procrastination. It helps us to prioritize as expected by the one who gives us the privilege of life and that was what I believe Jesus was indicating in the scripture. It would be a great loss and impact for example, to postpone an evangelistic opportunity and privilege to minister healing to the sick. As a matter of fact, any time you find yourself among the sick or under-privileged, see yourself as an extension of God's hand to bring a positive change into the life of the person or persons. There's no need to postpone the time and opportunity because no second opportunity is the same as the first. Neither is any errand better than an opportunity to minister healing or salvation to an available soul.

In Acts 3 for example, when Peter and John were going into the temple and met the lame man at the beautiful gate, they took the time available, to minister Christ to him and that brought the man his needed permanent change in life as against the temporary money he was expecting. Yes, sometimes what you may be expecting is not what you primarily need. So God in His manifold, wisdom fixes you with what you need spiritually and then proceeds to what you want, which is mostly physical. What is the difference? Needs are imperatives, wants are nice to haves. Now, Peter and John did not postpone the time and opportunity available, to 'after temple' or 'after church service' as some of us might have done and probably still do. Night is coming when no man can work! Also if they thought that way, who knows? Not only could they have missed him but the available and ripped time would have also passed. It is amazing how many of us Christians would prioritise our religious errands over dying souls and those in bondage. We need the confidence of God's presence and the power of the Holy Spirit to work with us.

When God took Ezekiel into the valley of dry bones in Ezekiel 37, it was not for a mere exhibition but for Ezekiel to command and bring life into lifeless situations. Given a similar opportunity, I can imagine how easy it would be to spot the difficulty and impossibility. However Solomon advises in scripture that:

He that observeth the wind shall not sow; and he that regardeth the clouds shall not reap. Eccl 11:4 KJV

Another great man of political leadership puts it this way:

A pessimist sees the difficulty in every opportunity; an optimist sees the opportunity in every difficulty.   **Winston Churchill**

Now bear in mind that it was the spirit of God who took Ezekiel into the valley and it was God who caused him to walk among and assess the dry bones. The Spirit of God spoke to him and asked him, can these bones live? These scenarios all mean that God was present with him and that alone should be an encouragement for a result because the bible says, that with God, nothing shall be impossible. What an assurance!

I have held the opinion that 'with God nothing shall be impossible' has two meanings. One is, '*God being in partnership with*' and two, '*as far as God is concerned*'. So if God was in partnership with him, then power for change was automatically with him, and therefore results was technically with him. It all has to do with who your partner is. Very similar to the case of the disciples in the boat amidst the storm in Mark 4:38! If God is in partnership with you and you know and believe it, then don't wait till the night when no man can work. Don't wait till you lose the needed ability. Whatever needs doing must be done at the earliest opportunity which is the time Jesus refers to as '*day*' and this certainly includes Healing and any form of service that meets a need and brings glory to God, our partner. Healing is a 'ready' ministry.

When I look back at my own life, I realise the numerous opportunities I had missed to share God's word with friends who are now unfortunately, out of my reach. I have missed many other opportunities to minister healing to others, but I have learnt and I am still learning.

The issue of good prioritisation would always surface when the resource of time is mentioned. This is because the effect can be so regrettable. That is why I believe Jesus does not want it to be taken for granted, as it is a fact.

One of the major threats and enemies to timely work for the Christian is the desire of the flesh for comfort and satisfaction over that of the spirit. When we take a refresher on Jesus's situation at the time when he met the boy born blind, he could have considered his personal safety (flesh) over the need of the blind boy's healing but no, he placed his spiritual responsibility first.

For the flesh desires what is contrary to the Spirit, and the Spirit what is contrary to the flesh. They are in conflict with each other, so that you are not to do whatever you want. Galatians 5:17 NIV

Every choice has a consequence and sometimes a series of consequences.

²⁹ Once when Jacob was cooking some stew, Esau came in from the open country, famished. ³⁰ He said to Jacob, "Quick, let me have some of that red stew! I'm famished!" (That is why he was also called Edom.[d]) ³¹ Jacob replied, "First sell me your birthright." ³² "Look, I am about to die," Esau said. "What good is the birthright to me?" ³³ But Jacob said, "Swear to me first." So he swore an oath to him, selling his birthright to Jacob. ³⁴ Then Jacob gave Esau some bread and some lentil stew. He ate and drank, and then got up and left.

So Esau despised his birthright. - Gen 25:29-34 NIV

It is a known and widely shared fact that Esau made a choice based on the demand of his flesh. He was in so much haste to gratify the flesh that all reasoning, consideration and reflections on consequences went out of the window. As he began to see death or the threat of it staring at him, he no longer saw anything good in the birthright. Jesus similarly starred people threatening to stone him, yet he did not despise the opportunity to serve and work. So we have two opposite choices. The consequence of Esau's choice is an example of what Jesus warned the disciples about and for that matter every Christian. That, a time is coming when no man can work. No man means, no man! An absolutely irrevocable circumstance regardless of effort.

¹⁶ That no one may become guilty of sexual vice, or become a profane (godless and sacrilegious) person as Esau did, who sold his own birthright for a single meal. ¹⁷ For you understand that later on, when he wanted [to regain title to] his inheritance of the blessing, he was rejected (disqualified and set aside), for he <u>could find no opportunity to repair</u> by repentance [what he had done, <u>no chance to recall the choice he had made</u>], although he sought for it carefully with [bitter] tears. Hebrews 12:16 -17 AMP

We can gather from the above scripture that, there are times and choices that cannot be undone no matter the efforts and bitter tears that accompany it. It is imperative that we make haste while the sun shines because the sun does not shine forever. Esau's tears did not bring back the opportunity he had lost.

When the blessing was bestowed on Jacob, Esau's brother in patriarchal manner, it was unalterable. Now, here is the point for us as Christians. Esau lived on the fringe of spiritual concern. Therefore, he lost out on the blessing, and it was regrettably, unchangeable. This teaches us that, if we live for the moment, with a rather light appreciation for the Christian inheritance and the blood that bought it, we can also lose our opportunity, and there is no second chance. There is no other way, no use for tears, no chance for repentance. As Bible says, it is appointed unto man once to die and after that judgement.

A further illustration can be deducted from the parable of the ten virgins in Matthew 25. Both wise and foolish virgins had the same opportunity and time to take extra oil. The wise ones used the available time and opportunity but the others did not. Unfortunately the time was not redeemable so the opportunity and hopes that the foolish ones had consequently became shattered.

[10] *"But while they were on their way to buy the oil, the bridegroom arrived. The virgins who were ready went in with him to the wedding banquet. And the door was shut.* Matthew 25:10 NIV

The Bible says the Virgins who were *ready* went in. It cannot be over emphasised that change can be on the way and just next door but the element of readiness is so important. Although all the virgins hoped to go to the Wedding Banquet with the bridegroom, only the wise who made use of the time to take an extra oil that went in. Time is a precious commodity and must be used wisely because it would make a difference between missing your change and meeting your change. May you meet your change!

Furthermore, like the rich man who became sorry once he was in torment, it was too late for him to repent and warn his brethren (Luke 16:19-31). This kind of regret comes too late and Jesus is saying, such times do come and will come, therefore do not postpone what can be done today to the next day. Change is on the way but please don't miss it through procrastination.

'Procrastination is the thief of time.'

>   Edward Young *English poet (1683 - 1765)*

CHAPTER 6

THE MASTER CHEMIST

(After saying this, he spit on the ground, made some mud with the saliva, and put it on the man's eyes.)

In our principal Passage of John 9:1-9, we see Christ performing a strange but miraculous chemical composition. He mixes mud and spit then applies it on the boy's eyes. Wow, what a chemical formulae! This is what I describe as the miraculous coming out of the ridiculous! He is the same man who turned water into wine at the wedding at Cana. As part of this section, I would like to detour to that story a bit, so we can learn more about resources and positioning when it comes to Jesus's miraculous chemistry. Amen.

Jesus changes the ordinary to the extra ordinary and always moves to save from shame and disgrace to establishing in glory and splendour.

The LORD will restore the splendor of Jacob like the splendor of Israel, though destroyers have laid them waste and have ruined their vines. - Nahum 2:2

Rescue from Shame

When Hope is in Place Shame is Displaced – Bishop N. A. Tackie-Yarboi

God is always ready to shine His glory through any creation. He uses the foolish things of this world to confound the wise. In Luke Chapter 5 Jesus confounded Peter, a professional fisherman who had exhausted all his fishing experiences and expertise without any result on one fishing night, with the same resources including the same sea. By a few words He directed Peter to a miraculous catch. He turned Peter's mourning of that night, into a morning of dancing! He shone His glory through Peter's disgraceful experience. What a dimension of healing, what a change! The key requirement was availability. Not ability!

Peter had the fishing ability, experience and resources. However in order to see the miracle from the loving Lord, he had to not just avail his boat as resource for Christ to use as a pulpit, but also be available to receive and conceive the instruction of Jesus. Obedience is an asset of availability.

At the wedding at Cana, Christ the master chemist, elucidates the power of availability over ability even more. Out of this fantastic story, I would like us to extract some juicy lessons about the power of availability over ability and even, purpose.

JOHN 2:1-11

On the third day a wedding took place at Cana in Galilee. Jesus' mother was there, ² and Jesus and his disciples had also been invited to the wedding. ³ When the wine was gone, Jesus' mother said to him, "They have no more wine."

⁴ "Woman,[a] why do you involve me?" Jesus replied. "My hour has not yet come." ⁵ His mother said to the servants, "Do whatever he tells you."

⁶ Nearby stood six stone water jars, the kind used by the Jews for ceremonial washing, each holding from twenty to thirty gallons. ⁷ Jesus said to the servants, "Fill the jars with water"; so they filled them to the brim. ⁸ Then he told them, "Now draw some out and take it to the master of the banquet."

They did so, ⁹ and the master of the banquet tasted the water that had been turned into wine. He did not realize where it had come from, though the servants who had drawn the water knew. Then he called the bridegroom aside ¹⁰ and said, "Everyone brings out the choice wine first and then the cheaper wine after the guests have had too much to drink; but you have saved the best till now." ¹¹ What Jesus did here in Cana of

Galilee was the first of the signs through which he revealed his glory; and his disciples believed in him.

Invitation Is Necessary

(Jesus and his disciples had also been invited)

In the above verse of the scripture we realise that Jesus and His disciples had been invited. Our Lord and Saviour does not gate crush, he shows up by appointment and when he shows up miracles follow. Simon the Pharisee in Luke 7, invited Jesus to his home but unfortunately not for the right reasons of entertaining and honouring him but rather, to test him for his prophetic gift and ministry and also, to assess his credibility as a man of God.

You cannot benefit from the grace of our Lord Jesus Christ if your motive for inviting him is wrong. If your invitation honours the Lord, you would reap a harvest of honour from him.

I can imagine how glad the wedding couple at Cana became, when they realised the value and quality of that invitation and indeed, the salvation and change it brought along with it.

A Desperate Situation

("They have no more wine.")

Desperate situations call for desperate measures and when it comes to healing and change in general, it is no different. Sometimes we need to be desperate in order to grasp our healing and experience the love and grace of God. Until the wine runs out, reality does not hit home. The wine has to run out for us to realise that what we thought to be the best, was not that good to begin with.

In a desperate situation you realize that what you thought was much was in fact, not enough to start with.

We can realize in the story that the quantity of wine was ridiculous to the task set before it. Very similar to the feeding of five thousand parable, recorded in Matthew 14:15-21:

15 As evening approached, the disciples came to him and said, "This is a remote place, and it's already getting late. Send the crowds away, so they can go to the villages and buy themselves some food." 16 Jesus replied, "They do not need to go away. You give them something to eat." 17 "We have here only five loaves of bread and two fish," they answered.

18 "Bring them here to me," he said. 19 And he directed the people to sit down on the grass. Taking the five loaves and the two fish and looking up to heaven, he gave thanks and broke the loaves. Then he gave them to the people. 20 They all ate and were satisfied, and the disciples picked up twelve basketfuls of broken pieces that were left over.

21 The number of those who ate was about five thousand men, besides women and children.

Five loaves of Bread and two fishes was a ridiculous menu before over five thousand hungry people.

You also begin to realize something very important. When the wine runs out, eyes open up to better direction. When the wine was available and everybody was enjoying, nobody probably noticed nor paid much attention to Mary, Jesus' mother. However, when the wine ran out they knew who to turn to, for directions. This is a typical picture of many of us and God. As long as things are as we wish and expect, we forget His omnipresence. We do what we like, when we like and how we like until desperation sets in. It is then, that we start looking for the presence which has always been with us. As Jacob said in Genesis 28, *God was here and I did not know it.*

The desperate widow in 2 Kings 4 had to look for Elisha when faced with the threat of losing her sons to her late husband's creditors and to avoid the shame that was knocking at her door. When she located the man of God, her story changed by a miraculous process that transformed her from a debtor to an entrepreneur, through a simple instruction from God through the prophet. Your story is about to change too, in Jesus name!

In desperate situations our spirit become more open to the voice, revelation and direction of God and we further, stabilise our dependency on Him.

Those who look to him are radiant; their faces are never covered with shame. Psalm 34:5 NIV

Zachaeus was desperate to catch a glimpse of Jesus so he climbed a tree. Desperation ignites our intentions into actions. He was desperate because he had run out of options for fulfilment. He had become rich from his work as a tax collector and more. However, he had run out of fulfilment and what he needed was a refill or a new fill. Therefore, Zachaeus climbs a tree in order to tap from the glimpse of the passing Jesus but that would not do. He needed a direct encounter with the master. His breakthrough came when he obeyed divine instruction. 'Zachaeus, Come down'.

The best way to connect with the Lord is in your 'coming down' rather than 'climbing up'. The process and image of coming down is indicative of humility and need and that is the exact point at which the Lord meets us; at our points of need.

In Mark 5, the woman with an issue of blood was desperate for her healing, desperate for her change. She had to bend or bow down in the process of touching the hem of Jesus's garment, signifying a posture of humility and worship. She encountered her change and had her healing. Your healing by change is indeed on the way and as you humble yourself and magnify the Lord in worship, may you receive it in Jesus name!

As we gather, after a short period over diner, Zachaeus became refilled with the 'new wine' of Jesus which made the 'old wine' so worth-less that, he was prepared to discount it into quadruples.

[8] But Zacchaeus stood up and said to the Lord, "Look, Lord! Here and now I give half of my possessions to the poor, and if I have cheated anybody out of anything, I will pay back four times the amount." – Luke 19:8 NIV

Merry making

It is worth mentioning that when the bible says '*they have no more wine*', merry making and pleasure had technically come to an end. Why? The Bible says:

[19] A feast is made for laughter, and wine <u>maketh merry</u>: but money answereth all things. Eccl. 10:19

The above scripture safely supports that, the guests at the Cana wedding had come to the end of their cheers, happiness and pleasure.

However, there is a much better source of happiness and this source is Jesus! He provides happiness that is better than the type that we have always known and he provides the best wine when the better wine runs out. He provides the Supernatural wine, when the natural wine runs out and to be quite candid, sometimes it takes a little bit of desperation to experience such testimonies. May you receive your own testimony in Jesus name!

The bible says that a merry heart heals like medicine. In other words, absence of 'the best wine' is a healing-less state which is sickness, illnesses, depression, etc. but the God of all grace supernaturally brings joy unspeakable. The story of Abraham and Sarah's desperation for a child illustrates this joy and pleasure nicely.

*Now Abraham and Sarah were old and well stricken in age; and **it ceased to be with Sarah** after the manner of women. Therefore Sarah laughed within herself, saying, After I am waxed old shall I have **pleasure**, my lord being old also? – Gen 18:11-12 KJV*

The Scripture said it *ceased to be with Sarah after the manner of women*. It meant that nature had run its course with her. This was just like the wine naturally running out as would normally be expected, when consumption exceeds provision, but the gracious thing is that, it might have ceased to be with Sarah after the manner of women but not ceased with her after the manner of God and for that reason, Sarah could have that supernatural pleasure which is only engineered by the God of Love and grace.

Sarah's best wine, was Isaac. Your best is on the way too! It might have ceased to be with you in the manner of nature but not ceased with the God of the supernatural. Your change is on the way!

You don't need to waste your time on the old wine because Jesus supernaturally provides the new wine! If you are in any form of deficiency, physically or emotionally, Jesus is your best bet, Jesus is the answer. You can have pleasure again and it shall be the best of pleasures, it shall be the best of joy and a highlight of testimonies in Jesus name!

CHAPTER 7

DIVINE APPOINTMENT
("My hour has not yet come.")

Time is of essence when it comes to experiencing and appreciating God's grace for change in healing and the glory that comes with making a difference. The glory that came upon the six stone water jars at the wedding at Cana, was time based. It was because they were available, empty or partially empty at a time when they were required to be so. Likewise although Jesus had probably been at the banquet from the beginning, he did not have to produce new wine at the beginning, not even at the time when his mother approached him regarding the situation, but at the hour, when divine timing and divine clock said so.

The Love of God is constant but His miracles including even breath of life is to do with His divine clock. So for the miracles of God to be experienced, the time has to come by divine appointment.

Divine Appointment

In 2 Kings 17:9, God told Elijah the Prophet to go to Zarephath in the region of Sidon, and that He had commanded a widow by divine appointment, to feed him there. This was just as the brook from which Elijah was drinking for survival dried up! God runs in when you run out!

Jesus respected and valued the accorded time from the father and did not move until it was up. It is important to understand God's timing. It minimises over anxiety, impatience and unnecessary frustration. However, when the divine clock hits your time, everything falls into place and it proves to be struggle free.

I remember when I was working towards acquiring my indefinite Stay in the UK. I applied every legal formulae available and possible but I was not successful. It was as if the whole world was fighting against me and my application. Friends who arrived in the UK years after me had their breakthroughs ahead of me. In some cases, I even advised them of the possible legal routes to gain indefinite. It worked for them perfectly and easily but not me. I spent money on fees, Solicitors etc. it never worked for me. It came to a time that I decided not to bother with it any longer so I will just focus on serving God. One day I went to Midweek church service. A leaflet about changes in the Immigration law for families had been laid on the seats. I took one home and based on the contents and provision of the leaflet, I made an application to the home office myself. The whole application cost me £2.80. Yes, two pounds and eighty pence, including recorded delivery fees! As cheap and easy as that. The rest is history.

I realised that the moment my focus shifted from Indefinite Stay to the Infinite God the divine clock begun to tick towards my favour. It was then that I moved. My time had come, easy and struggle free. May the divine clock of God begin to tick fast and towards your favour too in Jesus name!

Obedience is Key

("Do whatever he tells you.")

Obedience seems very simple but unfortunately it is the biggest issue God seems to have had with the men of old and as a matter of fact, humanity in general. It is a master key in every healing and positive difference.

God told Isaac:

*I will make your descendants as numerous as the stars in the sky and will give them all these lands, and through your offspring[a] all nations on earth will be blessed,[b] 5 **because** Abraham **obeyed** me and **did everything I required** of him, keeping my commands, my decrees and my instructions." –* Genesis 26:4-5 NIV

From the above scripture we clearly see Isaac and his descendants being beneficiaries of Abraham's obedience. It follows that our obedience can have a remote impact of blessings on our generations. The implicit opposite is also true of disobedience.

Obedience is not about nodding, but rather about doing. It is not just about doing either, but actually, doing everything required. So obedience is like a set menu rather than a buffet table, where you get to choose what you like and are ok with, leaving out what is inconvenient, uncomfortable and maybe unpleasant.

As a matter of fact, obedience becomes disobedience when accompanied with complain or even delay. In John 4:46-53, Bible gives a great and powerful meaning to obedience:

46 So Jesus came again into Cana of Galilee, where he made the water wine. And there was a certain nobleman, whose son was sick at Capernaum.

47 When he heard that Jesus was come out of Judaea into Galilee, he went unto him, and besought him that he would come down, and heal his son: for he was at the point of death.

48 Then said Jesus unto him, Except ye see signs and wonders, ye will not believe. 49 The nobleman saith unto him, Sir, come down ere my child die. 50 Jesus saith unto him, Go thy way; thy son liveth. And the man believed the word that Jesus had spoken unto him, and he went his way.

51 And as he was now going down, his servants met him, and told him, saying, Thy son liveth.

⁵² Then enquired he of them the hour when he began to amend. And they said unto him, yesterday at the seventh hour the fever left him.

⁵³ So the father knew that it was at the same hour, in which Jesus said unto him, Thy son liveth: and himself believed, and his whole house. - KJV

In the above story, we establish that the obedience of the nobleman's encounter with Jesus had been ignited by what he heard. He had heard that Jesus, the master scientist was in town. He had lent his ears to encouraging and positive news of testimony. This tells us that good news facilitates obedience to instruction, which can obviously lead to a miraculous breakthrough and desirable change.

We notice in the fiftieth verse above that, the obedience of the nobleman was subsequent to believing the word of Jesus which came in the form of instruction requiring obedience; *Go Thy Way*. The nobleman's obedience was in the form of action without a question nor remark unlike the verse number 49, where after Jesus had spoken in 48, the nobleman also spoke. This confirms that Obedience is an act of doing (*whatever he tells you to do, do it!*)

A miracle is born when man's obedience marries God's instruction.

So we see from the verse 51 above that, as he was on his way back home, he met his servants who told him the good news. As you read this book may you hear a desired good news in Jesus name!

What makes it even more beautiful is the fact that, he did not have to reach home in order to experience and testify of the power and authority in Jesus' word. He was met with the evidence. May that which God has spoken concerning any situation in your life come alive and be evident in Jesus name!

It is worth observing and noting that, on asking when the child had regained his health, the nobleman realised that it was the same hour that Jesus spoke the previous day. It confirms that, the word of God is accurate, sharper than a two edged sword and instant in season. There was basically no delay whatsoever. It was the same time!

The Element of Faith

Faith cannot be ruled out in a person's desire to see change in his or her life, especially when the situation seems hopeless and the clock is also ticking fast.

I cannot help but admire the nobleman's faith which was probably the substance that drove him to go such a long journey for what turned out to be probably no more than a 10 minutes conversation. It was at least a day's long journey! When you have so much faith distance means nothing.

I don't think it would take such a long time to travel that distance today. It follows that, what made the nobleman's journey that long was his mode of transport rather than the physical distance.

Now considering that he was a nobleman would have even meant, travelling by the fastest and most luxurious means available to him, yet it took him so long. Healing was the change he needed for his child and his faith drove him regardless of the distance to where healing was. Healing is on the way for you today and your change is here to stay!

It's rather unfortunate that in this day and age, some people would not take the pain to go to church for example, if their means of transport was challenged. They would not take the available lower option. In fact if it continues that way, they might even decide to change churches or stop church totally. Don't let convenience over rule your faith.

To further substantiate, obedience, a fruit of faith was what ended the toil of Peter and his fellow fishermen. *He said, nevertheless at thy word...* and when obedience married instruction, the same sea that yielded no fishes yielded more than enough. The same net that did not catch any fish earlier, caught more than it could handle. The fishermen who could not catch any fish previously, caught more than they could manage and therefore had to call for help in handling the catch. May God bring you a testimony of more than enough, as you exercise obedience to divine instructions, in Jesus name!

Obedience is such an important ingredient in seeing change manifest in your life. In Jeremiah 35 for example, a story is recorded about a group of people called the Recabites which formed an illustration of how disappointed God was with Israel concerning their disobedience. Disobedience disappoints God but obedience encourages God.

At the wedding in Cana, if the servants had not done what Jesus told them to do, the consequence would not have been the same. Obedience matters in miracles! Obedience matters if we would have personal testimonies of the unchanging God of change.

You must understand the timing of God in order to realise and appreciate it. May you co-operate with God when His clock ticks towards your direction to favour you. Your change is on the way and you shall not miss it!

CHAPTER 8

AVAILABILITY NOT ABILITY

(Nearby stood six stone water jars,)

The need of availability for the purpose of healing and any positive gracious change cannot be over-emphasized. At the wedding of Cana, the six stone water jars demonstrated this perfectly in relation to mankind. Why do I say that?

The number six here is not by chance nor accident but I believe it had a divine significance in the situation of these water Jars. Firstly, the number six symbolises the number for man, because man was created on the sixth day and for that reason there is a good message to mankind, which the Jars present. Since man was created for a divine purpose it goes without argument that the jars were also six for a divine purpose. You will not miss your divine purpose!

Secondly, six represents labour. Six days was man appointed to work (Exodus 34:21). Therefore I believe that the Stone water Jars being six in number was a hidden statement to demonstrate the effect of God's favour over man's labour. It takes time to brew wine and for the quality that turned out, God was surely making a statement to man, that when His favour comes upon you, it overwrites and overshadows a number of years of labour by divine acceleration! That will be your story in Jesus Name!

Thirdly the scripture says that they *Stood*, which to me was an indication of stability and dependability. It follows that stability is necessary in availability and that is what God requires. Ability to stand by faith. Shammah the third of David's mighty men, demonstrates this nicely:

*And after him was Shammah the son of Agee the Hararite. And the Philistines were gathered together into a troop, where was a piece of ground full of lentiles: and the people fled from the Philistines. ¹² But **he stood** in the midst of the ground, and defended it, and slew the Philistines: and the LORD wrought a great victory.* 2 Sam 23:11-12 KJV

There are believers that would flee at the very least opposition, challenge and difficulties but there are those like Shammah (*means 'Is There'*) who live up to the meaning of their names, who would loyally stand with you, stand for you and of course, for the gospel! I am talking about those with the attribute of God, on whom you can depend, because you can guarantee they would be there like Jehovah-Shammah (Ezek. 48:35)! These are the ones through whom the Lord brings victories. No wonder, the God of principles brought victory over shame, through the water jars. They 'Stood'! May you stand in availability too in Jesus name and may victory become your constant change!

Fourthly, the six stone water Jars were nearby. It means that the ease of access and reach play a vital role in availability, especially the reachability. Having a state of the art mobile phone in an area with no network makes a person unreachable and therefore unavailable. So circumstances can affect availability but in the case of the water jars, there was no issue. They were reachable and within coverage area.

The concept and matter of availability is easily assumed and therefore, easily confused. It is easy to assume that presence implies availability; but not quite so. It is therefore important to differentiate presence from availability. What do I mean?

The fact that a person or object is present is not an indication of availability. In my view, availability must satisfy the test of stability and readiness. For example a manager or consultant may clearly be in his or her office but if not ready to take consultation, he or she is unavailable even though, present. In the scripture above, the six stone water jars were available because they satisfied the test and measurement of 'stability'. The bible narrates that they *stood nearby*. In other words they were present where required and also accessible if required. God would only use instruments that are available even though not necessarily acceptable nor purposefully suitable.

It is a blessing to benefit from the power of God to change but you have to be available. You must be there when required and there if needed!

Many people have missed this blessing as instruments and extension of God's hand because of inconsistency in their availability. They are mostly present, but unfortunately, absent on the day and at the time when they were mostly needed. Consistency underlines availability and inconsistency robs of blessing.

A very good illustration of consistency is seen in the Story of the man at the pool of Bethesda found in John 5:1-9 KJV:

⁵ And a certain man <u>was there</u>, which had an infirmity thirty and eight years. ⁶ When Jesus saw him lie, and knew that he had been now a long time in that case, he saith unto him, Wilt thou be made whole?

It can be deduced from the scripture that the man had been going to the pool year after year. However, he never encountered the change, healing and miracle he was desiring until the thirty-eighth year of his visit. His consistency is what underlined his availability for healing, a change he had obviously desired for a very long time. The Bible says 'a certain man *was there*'. His name was not mentioned, but what mattered was that, he *was there*! It is very easy to miss out on healing and your desired change due to inconsistency which unfortunately can render you unavailable.

The man had been attending the pool probably before Jesus was born. He had been in the condition for thirty-eight years whiles his deliverer, Jesus himself, lived for only 33 ½ years. So had he not been there that particular day or festival, he would have missed this special visitation and blessing of healing packaged and prepared for him as part of Jesus's project plan, right from birth! Your change is coming and your healing is on the way but your consistency would help.

We can imagine how many good Christians have missed their visitations because they were not in Church on the day the Lord visited specially for them. How many decided to quit their ministries and church functions because their healing or expectation had delayed from manifesting? It is worth mentioning that, endurance fuels and equips consistency during seasons of persistent disappointments. You need to endure disappointments knowing that, your change is coming. This man at the pool of Bethesda must have exercised great endurance over years of disappointments, but he still expected his change. He did not miss it!

We serve a living God, the God of love, change and miracles who heals and makes all things beautiful in His own time to an extent that, it is easier than comprehensible.

For this is what the LORD says: You will see neither wind nor rain, yet this valley will be filled with water, and you, your cattle and your other animals will drink. This is <u>an easy thing</u> in the eyes of the LORD; he will also deliver Moab into your hands. 2 Kings 3:17 -18 NIV

Change and healing in general is an easy thing in the eyes of God!

There are cases where probably the choir master or chief usher had told a person off for misconduct, after yet an admirable and applaudable consistency in service. Or, on a particular day, especially when a major programme has been organised and their service and participation was of high requirement, decided to absent themselves in order to prove their worth to their leader. In simple terms immaturity can erase a length of availability and rob you from experiencing a desired change in various dimensions. Paul said *'when I was a child, I spake as a child, I understood as a child, I thought as a child: but when I became a man, I put away childish things.'* (1 Cor.13:11). It follows that there are certain changes that would not be appreciated until there have been some form of anatomical and mental changes and reshuffles; until a whole paradigm has been shifted!

With the six stone water jars, the bible says they stood and were also *nearby*! They were available and accessible. Availability matters!

"The Lord doesn't ask about your ability, only your availability; and, if you prove your dependability, the Lord will increase your capability." (thinkexist.com)

Cost of Unavailability

Remembering the birth of Jesus, this glory that came upon the 6 stone water Jars could have similarly come upon the Inn where Jesus could have been born and if that had happened, you and I can imagine the additional fame and generational income the Inn could be attracting till this day through tourists visits. Unfortunately that day, there was no room in the Inn.

And she gave birth to her firstborn, a son. She wrapped him in cloths and placed him in a manger, because there was no guest room available for them. Luke 2:7 NIV

Sometimes I wonder whether there was honestly no room in the inn. Or was it one of those mistakes that some judgemental people and organisations make in our day and age today?

Now, assuming there was room, but looking at the appearance of a carpenter and a virgin from Nazareth, they were not in a position to meet the costs of the inn. Probably they did not fit-in with the celebrities that usually lodged there either. Therefore, they could have been given an excuse of 'no vacancy', in order to protect the inn's reputation. Now, these sorts of things do happen in our present society. I remember the film by Richard Gere and Julia Roberts called 'Pretty Woman'. How the hotel manager wished Julia could not be admitted to the hotel!

If this analysis was true, then what a miss this had been, for the greatest of all kings to have been born in that Inn! In a similar way, sometimes healing and for that matter any desired change would be on the way to a needing person, but the package and transport delivering the healing may be rejected and that becomes a long irrevocable loss. May you not miss your change and the everlasting testimony it brings.

Availability over function and purpose

(The kind used by the Jews for ceremonial washing)

The Stone water jars were for the purpose of ceremonial washing. However, their availability and dependability caused Christ to increase their capability to brewing wine.

As part of God's love, he transforms the neglected and the written offs. I can easily guess how these water jars were viewed with restriction of function and purpose. That's all they can do and that's as far as they can go! I wonder how many people imagined that the best ever wine would be brewed through water jars and not wine casks!

It follows that, it does not matter how people see you. What matters is how God sees you. God sees you according to your potential not your potency and he can use you over and beyond your capability, if you can be available!

Jeremiah saw himself as a local boy who could not speak but God saw him as an international Prophet (Jeremiah 1:3-6). Do not limit yourself to localised mentality because God has bigger plans and purposes for you that you cannot see.

Donkeys are not prophets but when it mattered God considered availability and increased the capability of Prophet Balaam's Donkey to prophetic ministry and deliverance.

Numbers 22:23-35 NIV

23 When the donkey saw the angel of the LORD standing in the road with a drawn sword in his hand, it turned off the road into a field. Balaam beat it to get it back on the road. 24 Then the angel of the LORD stood in a narrow path through the vineyards, with walls on both sides. 25 When the donkey saw the angel of the LORD, it pressed close to the wall, crushing Balaam's foot against it. So he beat the donkey again. 26 Then the angel of the LORD moved on ahead and stood in a narrow place where there was no room to turn, either to the right or to the left. 27 When the donkey saw the angel of the LORD, it lay down under Balaam, and he was angry and beat it with his staff. 28 Then the LORD opened the donkey's mouth, and it said to Balaam, "What have I done to you to make you beat me these three times?" 29 Balaam answered the donkey, "You have made a fool of me! If only I had a sword in my hand, I would kill you right now."

30 The donkey said to Balaam, "Am I not your own donkey, which you have always ridden, to this day? Have I been in the habit of doing this to you?" "No," he said. 31 Then the LORD opened Balaam's eyes, and he saw the angel of the LORD standing in the road with his sword drawn. So he bowed low and fell facedown. 32 The angel of the LORD asked him,

"Why have you beaten your donkey these three times? I have come here to oppose you because your path is a reckless one before me.[a] 33 The donkey saw me and turned away from me these three times. If it had not turned away, I would certainly have killed you by now, but I would have spared it."

The donkey was seen by her owner as only good for carriage and transportation but her availability at a time when deliverance was an emergency, caused God to use it beyond just a means of carriage.

May God use you beyond your tag and imagination, in Jesus name!

Emptiness Is Necessary

("Fill the jars with water")

In order to enjoy the love and miraculous move of God, we have to do away with the things that render us unemptied. The things that block our ability to receive and to produce. One of the subtle of these things that block our receptive ability is over-familiarity.

Over familiarity makes you look and feel so full, it tends to projects a message of *'I have no need'*. I am already full, I don't need any more teaching, I know it all, I have seen it all!

In Matthew 9:12 Jesus said: *"It is not the healthy who need a doctor, but the sick"*.

It follows that a sick person portraying not to need a doctor is a victim of self-deception and that, is dangerous. When you become over familiar and take God and the things of God for granted, you consequently become unavailable for the miraculous blessing of God. This includes being in Church, yet believing that you know more than the Pastor and he or she has nothing to teach you. Emptiness is a representation of a teachable spirit.

It is very difficult to learn when you feel you know it all and therefore nobody has and can teach you anything. Unfortunately, when you stop learning, you stop growing and when you stop growing, you start dying. May we learn and live in Jesus name!

A person cannot be available if he or she is not empty or ready. The Stone water Jars were available; they were not full and therefore had the room and capacity to be used.

Filling only comes when there's a demonstration of room, hunger and thirst. The Bible says that blessed are those who hunger and thirst after righteousness for they shall be filled. (Matt. 5:6).

Jesus asked the people at the Cana wedding banquet to fill the Jars with water. He was using what was available to bring about what was unavailable. Using the cheapest and commonest to bring forth the dearest and uncommon and at a point, when nobody thought there was any better on the way!

As God said to Habakkuk:

5 Behold ye among the heathen, and regard, and wonder marvellously: for I will work a work in your days which ye will not believe, though it be told you. Habakkuk 1:5 KJV

Your Best is yet to come because change is on the way!

Dangers of Over Familiarity

(The Michal and Uzzah Syndrome)

Overfamiliarity is a subtle character or spirit that has robbed many people of a change that could have positioned them for greatness and blessing. In some cases overfamiliarity has ended their lives prematurely.

Michal, David's wife missed out on David's blessing when out of over familiarity with her husband, despised him in her heart whiles David danced in front of the ark of God, heading home with an intention to bless his household.

"And as the ark of the LORD came into the city of David, Michal Saul's daughter looked through a window, and saw King David leaping and dancing before the LORD; and she despised him in her heart." 2 Samuel 6:16 KJV

Michal's over familiarity blinded her from the fact that her husband was not only anointed but was in the presence of God, praising and worshipping. She failed to think that, no matter how embarrassing an anointed man could be, he can still impart and impact!

Michal felt she knew best. She was not empty! She was not available to receive the blessing of David for his household. Her heart had been filled with despise and technically was sitting in the seat of the scornful!

"Blessed is the man that walketh not in the counsel of the ungodly, nor standeth in the way of sinners, nor sitteth in the seat of the scornful" (Psa. 1:1). KJV

Overfamiliarity can make you scornful. Unfortunately the seat of the scornful is not that of a blessing but rather the opposite. So an opportunity which could have made Michal partake of anointed King David's blessing unfortunately eluded her and rather resulted in her bareness. She missed her change. Overfamiliarity can be very dangerous without estimation!

Similarly, Uzzah touched the ark against the instruction of God. The ark had stumbled and was about to fall. Uzzah who was following it took a reflex action to save it from following and ended up being struck dead by God. As a most probable fact, the intention of Uzzah was right, but his action was wrong. In a similar vein, having a good point or intention does not necessarily give you a right of action. For example, David had a point and a reason to kill King Saul in the cave of Abdullah but had no right, because Saul was anointed.

"Do not touch my anointed ones; do my prophets no harm." – Psalm 105:15 NIV

Uzzah had probably become overfamiliar with the ark having been in their house for a period of 20 years (1 Sam 7:2), he had lost the difference of view between the ark and any other furniture in Abinadab's house. Question.... Could it be that Uzzah might have touched the Ark before but in private and behind closed doors, so he thought he could do the same in public? As the saying goes *'Charity begins at home '.*

Sometimes what grace would allow in private, the law would kick in and kick hard against it in public. We must be careful! The Lamb of God and the Lion of the tribe of Judah has not changed. Ananias and Sapphira for example, died in the era of grace due to overfamiliarity with God and His ways. Over familiarity can be very dangerous.

The Danger of Pride

Another dangerous thing that makes us unavailable for filling, is pride.

Live in harmony with one another. Do not be proud, but be willing to associate with people of low position. Do not be conceited. Rom 12:16 NIV

Pride can stop you from learning and therefore knowing more. It does not matter who you are or how much you know, always allow some room for extra knowledge. As previously said, when learning stops, growth seizes and when growth seizes retardation and degradation are inevitable.

24 Meanwhile a Jew named Apollos, a native of Alexandria, came to Ephesus. He was a learned man, with a thorough knowledge of the Scriptures. 25 He had been instructed in the way of the Lord, and he spoke with great fervor and taught about Jesus accurately, though he knew only the baptism of John. 26 He began to speak boldly in the synagogue. When Priscilla and Aquila heard him, they invited him to their home and explained to him the way of God more adequately. Acts 18:24-26 NIV

The Scripture above clearly states that Apollos was a learned man, with thorough knowledge of the scriptures and taught about Jesus *accurately.* He was a speaker or let's even say, a lecturer in the synagogue. However, it took tent makers like Priscilla and Aquila to give him *adequate* explanation of the way of the Lord. It follows that it is possible to be accurate and yet inadequate. Apollos was a lecturer but it was his emptiness that allowed him to be filled to adequacy by people of comparatively lower position. If you can be empty, you can be filled.

Pride is a well blocker and can obstruct your potential. Furthermore, God himself opposes the proud but He gives grace to the humble (1 Peter 5:5).

Pride goes before destruction, a haughty spirit before a fall. Prov. 16:18 NIV

CHAPTER 9

GET READY FOR A TESTIMONY

("Now draw some out and take it to the master of the banquet.")

When God makes and brings the best out of you, he positions you for a testimony to all. When Jesus cleansed the 10 lepers he asked them to show themselves to the priest in accordance with the law. Likewise, the first to taste, test and validate the wine was the master of the banquet and when he had finished, he commended and testified to all that, it was the best!

The enemy might threaten you with disgrace, but God will graciously reverse it!

May God bring the best out of you and place you visibly as a trophy of testimony!

The Role of Gratitude

One major key to elevations and testimonies is gratitude. It is your gratitude that determines your altitude. In the story of the ten lepers (Luke 17), Jesus cleansed ten lepers and asked them to go and show themselves to the priest in accordance with the law. However, on their way, one of them noticed a sign of cleansing and returned to Jesus, to say a big thank you. Now, that was a sign of a grateful person. He was grateful just for the sign.

If you can be grateful just for a sign, God will make you a sign and symbol of gratitude.

We don't know how far the lepers reached before noticing the sign. Probably a shorter distance to the priest than backwards to Christ, but that did not matter. He still took the pain to journey back to praise and say 'thank you' to Jesus, with the intention of making the Journey back to the priest for verification and validation as he was meant to do. However, when he had given thanks, he did not have to do the Journey a second time, because he had become whole, which is a change beyond his expectation of healing. A state that was obvious and needed no priest validation because the great high priest himself had declared wholeness!

It follows that your praise and gratitude can wipe off all kinds of debts even those in the form of sicknesses and diseases and it can also shorten lengthy journeys and processes.

Your heart of gratitude can shorten your journeys without adversely affecting your desired result. You could gain exemption from the normal course of events and applications because of your praise and gratitude.

Gratitude is an ease of a humble heart but pride despises beauty. When Jesus overthrew the tables of the money changers in the temple and went on to heal the blind and the lame, the chief priests and scribes were displeased but the humble children sang praises at the wonders they saw.

They asked Jesus, "Do you hear what these children are saying?" "Yes," Jesus replied. "Haven't you ever read the Scriptures? For they say, 'You have taught children and infants to give you praise.'" Matt 21:16 NLT

Increased Capability

(He did not realize where it had come from)

God is able to make a way where there seems to be no way and out of nothing He makes something. In a similar way as the wine, Samson brought honey from the carcass of a lion to feed himself and his parents. They did not know where it had come from. Nobody would expect to eat out of a lion, especially, a dead lion. The Bible says:

8 After some time, when he returned to get her, he turned aside to see the carcass of the lion. And behold, a swarm of bees and honey were in the carcass of the lion. 9 He took some of it in his hands and went along, eating. When he came to his father and mother, he gave some to them, and they also ate. But he did not tell them that he had taken the honey out of the carcass of the lion. Judges 14:8-9 KJV

Samson turned probably to remember his God-enabled victory over the lion and to trust him for another victory over hunger, a situation that had most probably confronted him at the time and lo, the God who provided him strength to overcome the lion, provided him food yet, out of the same lion.

I pray that like Samson, you would overcome any threat and attack that confronts you to the extent that it will rather become an advantage and provision for you, in Jesus name!

Now, if Samson's parents knew where the honey they were eating had come from, they would not have eaten it. They would probably have even thrown up not only in disgust but also to avoid contamination. Likewise, the Master of the Banquet at the wedding of Cana; because I can imagine the neglected external condition of the standing stone water jars and for that reason, presenting a rather unclean appearance.

It's also amazing to note how God protected Samson from the bees as they did not seem to have attacked him. It was a miracle similar to the ravens, feeding Elijah in 1 Kings 17:2 NIV.

2 Then the word of the LORD came to Elijah: 3 "Leave here, turn eastward and hide in the Kerith Ravine, east of the Jordan. 4 **You will drink from the brook, and I have ordered the ravens to feed you there."**

*5 So he did what the LORD had told him. He went to the Kerith Ravine, east of the Jordan, and stayed there. 6 **The ravens brought him bread and meat in the morning and bread and meat in the evening, and he drank from the brook.***

Law and Grace at Play

It is beautiful to observe the play of the Law and grace in the above scenarios. Under the law God gives an outline about the unclean birds in Deuteronomy 14:11-15 NIV, saying:

*11 You may eat any clean bird. 12 But these you may not eat: the eagle, the vulture, the black vulture, 13 the red kite, the black kite, any kind of falcon, 14 **any kind of raven**, 15 the horned owl, the screech owl, the gull, any kind of hawk,*

However, when it mattered and for the love of Elijah, God varied the Law under an exceptional circumstance that, he even commanded, an unclean bird to act in a clean capacity. This is Grace in action. Unmerited favour in action!

Under the law, if a clean person touches anything that was unclean the clean is infected by the unclean, making uncleanness infectious under the law. However, Holiness is not infectious under the Law.

In the book of Haggai 2:10-13 KJV:

10 In the four and twentieth day of the ninth month, in the second year of Darius, came the word of the LORD by Haggai the prophet, saying, 11 Thus saith the LORD of hosts; Ask now the priests concerning the law, saying, 12 If one bear holy flesh in the skirt of his garment, and with his skirt do touch bread, or pottage, or wine, or oil, or any meat, shall it be holy? And the priests answered and said, No. 13 Then said Haggai, if one that is unclean by a dead body touch any of these, shall it be unclean? And the priests answered and said, it shall be unclean.

Every single bit of food that came to Elijah, came from the beak of a Raven and therefore would have been technically infected by the uncleanness. Now, as Elijah was a strict Jew this feeding process would have required him to put away his traditional ideas and values of clean and unclean animals as well as clean and unclean people otherwise, he would have died out of starvation.

A similar incident would possibly have occurred to Samson's parents whiles at the wedding at Cana, the master of ceremony would have suffered a total disgrace rather than the Bride and Groom. This is because the proper management of the Wedding Banquet was the responsibility of the master of the banquet or more popularly, master of ceremony (MC) and not the couple.

Through this, I believe God was teaching Elijah to emphasize the *spirit of the law* before the *letter of the law*. The Spirit of the Law is of Intention and purpose, whereas the Letter of the Law is as raw and straight forward as it is written.

Charles Spurgeon, drew two points of application from this event, likening the food the ravens brought to spiritual food.

Firstly, Spurgeon recognized that God may bring a good word to us through a vessel which is spiritually unclean, just like a raven. Secondly, that a person or let's even say, a pastor can bring good spiritual food to others and still be spiritually unclean herself or himself. As he said:

"But see, too, how possible it is for us to carry bread and meat to God's servants, and do, some good things for his church, and yet be ravens still!" (Spurgeon)

So the beauty of Grace must have kicked in here and likewise at the wedding Banquet because under grace, it is not uncleanness which is contagious but rather Holiness. 1Cor 7:12-14 says:

[12] To the rest I say this (I, not the Lord): If any brother has a wife who is not a believer and she is willing to live with him, he must not divorce her. [13] And if a woman has a husband who is not a believer and he is

willing to live with her, she must not divorce him. ¹⁴ *For the unbelieving has been sanctified through his wife, and the unbelieving wife has been sanctified through her believing husband. Otherwise your children would be unclean, but as it is, they are holy.*

So effectively due to the loving grace of God, Samson's honey from the Lion's Carcass (Deut. 14:21) had been sanctified for his consumption simply by the contact of his hand, likewise the Raven's food to Elijah. In the same capacity, the unworthiness of the stone water jars had been made worthy by the Master's choice to expand their capability to brewing the best wine. Consequently, they gained more respect and recognition. May the grace of God elevate you over laws and traditions and cause your profile to rise. May you gain more respect and recognition as change makes its way to you, in Jesus name.

I am sure that if the Master of the Banquet knew where the best wine had come from, he would never under-estimate nor look down on anything and anybody especially if he knew the extent of God's miraculous ability. God is able to transform anybody and anything by grace and this is one of the major reasons why you should not despise anybody.

I remember a message my Spiritual father, Bishop Clement preached years back. He titled it 'The Value of People'. This was the message that made me decide to commit to his spiritual tutelage and to Victory Bible Church. He stressed not to despise people. He elaborated through his personal story in relation to his wife and humble beginnings and another scenario, on a church testimony platform as a child. It re-echoed the spirit my biological father had planted in me; to love and value people.

God's grace is always sufficient even in hopeless circumstances. His grace will sponsor and support your change so no matter what, be strong and expectant. Change is on the way so get ready for a testimony!

CHAPTER 10

BEST FOR LAST
(But you have saved the best till now.")

The God of change and miracles displaces Shame. No matter the threat of disgrace God will graciously reverse it. Sometimes it may seem long and delayed but God will show up. He has a time called *His time* and it is at this time that He makes *everything* beautiful, not some things, but everything!

He hath made everything beautiful in his time: also he hath set the world in their heart, so that no man can find out the work that God maketh from the beginning to the end. Eccl 3:11

At the wedding of Cana, the Master of the Banquet commended the Groom for saving the best wine to the last, unlike most people. Yes, you are unique and not like everyone else so you don't have to fit the status quo, you are different and have a right to do things differently by the power and provision of God. You don't have to conform because you are a walking testimony of the transforming and changing power of the Most High God and therefore disgrace shall never have the better of you! God is our change engineer and he has not relinquished this divine profession.

King Solomon said 'better *is* the end of a thing than the beginning thereof: *and* the patient in spirit *is* better than the proud in spirit. '(Eccl 7:8).

In a similar way as Jesus wrought this miracle to overshadow the threatening shame with the best wine, so will He do in your life and circumstance! As Moses would put it according to Exodus 14:13, "Do not be afraid. Stand firm and you will see the deliverance the LORD will bring you today. The Egyptians you see today you will never see again". What I love about the assurance of God's word through Moses in this scripture is the lasting ability. It says the Egyptians you see, you shall not see again! The shame and disgraceful threats, you shall not experience again. The failed attempts in exams, failed interviews you have experienced, you shall not experience them again! The various forms of miscarriages and evil reports you shall not experience again, because God has saved your best till now!

There's an idiom that goes like '*He who laughs last laughs the longest and He who laughs last laughs best*! I prophecy that your laughter will be the best and it will also be the longest in Jesus name!

In the book of Genesis we read that Rachel whom Jacob loved went a long time without a child to the extent that, she was seriously desperate and began to put her trust into man and mandrakes. However, the God of love and miracles showed up with her change; Oh my God!

She became pregnant and gave birth to a son and said, "God has taken away my disgrace." Gen 30:23 NIV

In that same way, when the desperation showed up God took away the disgrace at the Wedding through the new wine. He is still in the business of taking away shame!

I must clarify that when Moses said '*Stand firm*', in Exodus 14:13, he was not literally referring to physical standing by strength and power, but by trusting God and keeping his statutes.

It is very easy to fold up and give up when situations become desperately tough but it is only when you have held on till the end that you see and appreciate the saving power and grace of God. As Shadrach, Meshach and Abednego held on to the decrees of the Lord, the faithful God showed up with salvation for them. He is the God of change but not a changing God. As he did for them He will do for you too.

Take insult and contempt away from me, for I have kept your decrees.
Psalm 119:22 (HCSB)

The Psalmist was able to claim his entitlement to change based on the fact that he had kept the decrees of God. That was his point of reference and legal article for change. If you would endeavour to keep His decrees, you can rightfully demand a change.

Prayer is a necessary change element

In a similar vein, when Hezekiah prayed for God to tamper justice with mercy concerning his death pronouncement, the Bible says in Isaiah chapter thirty-eight that 'Then Hezekiah turned his face toward the wall, and prayed to the LORD, and said, "Remember now, O LORD, I pray, *how I have walked before You in truth and with a loyal heart, and have done what is good in Your sight.*" And Hezekiah wept bitterly. God then sent Isaiah back with a gracious message to Hezekiah that, He had heard his prayer and had added fifteen years (Intensified Grace) to his age. What a change?! The change in the directive of God was not based on Hezekiah's physical tears but rather the tears of his heart coupled with a prayer of legalistic references under the old covenant of Deuteronomy 28 and Leviticus 26.

However, today we are under the new wine and lasting grace of God through faith in Jesus so we don't have to necessarily pray like that, although it's not wrong. It is about what Christ has done for us and not what we have done or are doing ourselves because our righteousness is like filthy rags unto God and by strength shall no man prevail.

Now God being so gracious he brought about other changes necessary in the life of Hezekiah that were not even part of his prayer.

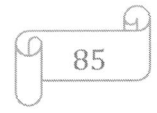

Now unto him that is able to do exceeding abundantly above all that we ask or think, according to the power that worketh in us, Eph. 3:20 KJV

During the fifteen extra years given to Hezekiah, his first son Manasseh was born to him in the third year. Which is why Manasseh became King at the age of twelve when his Dad died. It follows that, had Hezekiah not prayed, he would have died childless leaving the throne of David and line of Judah without the direct bloodline heir unto Christ but prayer came to make that change. Your prayer is important in your desired Change and even beyond.

I also wish to state that in God's instrumentation of change, there is no confusion. When God changed the prophecy concerning Hezekiah, He did not use a different prophet. He used the same Isaiah to return with the new and overriding decree. This way there was no ambiguity and confusion. Care must be exercised when differing and opposing messages are received from two prophets both claiming to have been sent by God. One of them would be lying.

God gave a word to a prophet for King Jeroboam and specifically warned him not to eat or drink anything after the mission, neither was he to take the same route as he went originally. However, another prophet came to him and asked him to come home with him, with a totally opposite message to what God had originally given him:

⁷ The king said to the man of God, "Come home with me for a meal, and I will give you a gift." ⁸ But the man of God answered the king, "Even if you were to give me half your possessions, I would not go with you, nor would I eat bread or drink water here. ⁹ For I was commanded by the word of the Lord: 'You must not eat bread or drink water or return by the way you came.'" ¹⁰ So he took another road and did not return by the way he had come to Bethel.

¹¹ Now there was a certain old prophet living in Bethel, whose sons came and told him all that the man of God had done there that day.

They also told their father what he had said to the king. ¹² Their father asked them, "Which way did he go?" And his sons showed him which road the man of God from Judah had taken. ¹³ So he said to his sons, "Saddle the donkey for me." And when they had saddled the donkey for him, he mounted it ¹⁴ and rode after the man of God. He found him sitting under an oak tree and asked, "Are you the man of God who came from Judah?" "I am," he replied. ¹⁵ So the prophet said to him, "Come home with me and eat." ¹⁶ The man of God said, "I cannot turn back and go with you, nor can I eat bread or drink water with you in this place. ¹⁷ I have been told by the word of the LORD: 'You must not eat bread or drink water there or return by the way you came.'"

¹⁸ The old prophet answered, "I too am a prophet, as you are. And an angel said to me by the word of the LORD: 'Bring him back with you to your house so that he may eat bread and drink water.'" (But he was lying to him.) ¹⁹ So the man of God returned with him and ate and drank in his house.

²⁰ While they were sitting at the table, the word of the LORD came to the old prophet who had brought him back. ²¹ He cried out to the man of God who had come from Judah, "This is what the LORD says: 'You have defied the word of the LORD and have not kept the command the LORD your God gave you. ²² You came back and ate bread and drank water in the place where he told you not to eat or drink. Therefore your body will not be buried in the tomb of your ancestors.'"

²³ When the man of God had finished eating and drinking, the prophet who had brought him back saddled his donkey for him. ²⁴ As he went on his way, a lion met him on the road and killed him, and his body was left lying on the road, with both the donkey and the lion standing beside it. ²⁵ Some people who passed by saw the body lying there, with the lion standing beside the body, and they went and reported it in the city where the old prophet lived. 1Kings 13:7-25 NIV

Always test the prophecy. In the lie prophecy, the Old Prophet said an angel had spoken to him. Why should the young prophet fall for a message of angels through a prophet when God himself had initially spoken to him directly? This is the point I was making. If God wanted to change the original instruction, He would have more than likely spoken to him directly as he did before not through someone else, thereby creating confusion. Amazingly, God still spoke to the old prophet but this time with a rather unfortunate message for the young prophet and a good awakening lesson to all of us. What a shock?! In your readiness to embrace your change be careful of contradictory prophecies.

Add a seed to your prayer

Similar to Hezekiah, it was Hannah's earnest prayer plus a prophetic seed in the form of a vow that brought about her change and long lasting laughter in her son, Samuel.

And she made a vow, saying, "LORD Almighty, if you will only look on your servant's misery and remember me, and not forget your servant but give her a son, then I will give him to the LORD for all the days of his life, and no razor will ever be used on his head." 1 Sam 1:11NIV

In her prayer, she was specific about her desired change. She did not ask for a child generally, she asked for a son. It is important to be specific even though God reserves the right to give you what He sees fit and in your best interest. As we know from this popular story, Hannah had the last and longest laugh over her revival Peninnah.

I must warn that, it is a dangerous thing to make fun of anybody using their unfortunate circumstance. Bible admonishes us to mourn with those who mourn and to rejoice with those who rejoice. Peninnah did exactly the opposite and she reaped an unfortunate harvest of change. It is a well-established record that after Chapter one of first Samuel, Peninnah's name did not surface explicitly in Scripture again. Implicitly she appears in Hannah's testimonial prayer in Chapter two

"The bows of the warriors are broken, but those who stumbled are armed with strength. ⁵ Those who were full hire themselves out for food, but those who were hungry are hungry no more. She who was barren has borne seven children, <u>but she who has had many sons pines away</u>. 1 Sam 2:4-5 NIV

From the above scripture we can possibly deduce that both Peninnah and her Children sadly faded away. A possible reason that we don't hear of Peninnah or any of her Children with Elkannah in subsequent scriptures. A rather negative change. May that not be your portion, in Jesus name!

Like the new wine at the wedding, God saved Hannah's best till last. She had Samuel, a very special son who she gave back to the Lord in honour of her vow and was replaced with five gracious Children in her home. *She who was barren has borne seven children.* I tend suspect that, she might have counted Elkannah her husband, as one of her children as most wives graciously like to consider us, their husbands.

Now, the Greek word for "best" is *kalos* which simply means good, right, beautiful, noble, and excellent. The wine Jesus produced at the wedding was seen as *'kalos'*. Now in Christ, we have the best of Life and have it even in abundance.

The Greek word for "salvation" is *sozo* which is a generic word meaning to save, rescue, deliver, heal and make whole. One of the best changes anybody could expect and experience is that of salvation, to which I believe the miraculous provision of the wine in saving from shame, graciously typifies. It means you don't have to go through the physical lengthy months to be born again nor vintage process of brewing wine to have the best. It is supernatural. Hallelujah!

God's best for you, in your life is here and that is for you to enjoy the best change of your life which are, His blessings and His victory for you via the cross of Calvary. Blessings to move you up in the power of the Holy Spirit and for you to see and be used for signs and wonders done in His name so that, souls like that of the man at the beautiful gate (Acts 3) will be saved and backsliders returned unto our Lord and saviour Jesus Christ.

Every good gift and every perfect gift is from above, and cometh down from the Father of lights, with whom is no variableness, neither shadow of turning ". James 1:17 KJV

Formerly, people used to put the old Sun Dial in their gardens in order to tell the time by the shadow of the sun. The power of the Sun is most intense when it hits 12 noon. However, the word of God elucidates to us that, at the peak of power, God does not change. He is always at the peak of His power, no shifting like shifting shadows. God is basically saying that, when he does something it is always at His best is unchangeable and un-negotiable.

By this first of Jesus' miraculous signs He performed in Cana of Galilee, He revealed his glory and his disciples put their faith in him. Similarly, Jesus has revealed his glory to us all by the work of grace and his ultimate sacrifice on the cross for our sins. At Calvary Jesus revealed his love for us all, by his death and resurrection. He effectively, revealed his glory to us. We now have a choice and a responsibility to put our faith in him who gave his best for us all. Praise the Lord!

It is important to mention that, one day there will be a wedding party, but this time in heaven rather than Cana and only those who have accepted Jesus as their Lord and personal saviour who will be at that great wedding feast. Only those who have accepted that invitation to "come unto him ", will be allowed in. My desire and prayer is that if you have not accepted him already, you will not miss out on what God has availed for you via the serving of new wine which is the new life in Christ Jesus. The Bible provides by Romans 10:9 that, if you declare with your mouth, "Jesus is Lord," and believe in your heart that God raised him from the dead, you will be saved.

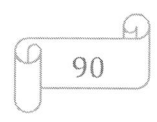

He has saved the best till now, just for you and me. You must not miss it. Halleluiah!

CHAPTER 11

CHANGE AND YOUR SACRIFICE

No Change, goal or achievement comes without a sacrifice. Every good thing comes at a price and usually an expensive one too. The God of love and miracles, for His love for this world and humanity gave his only begotten son as a sacrifice for the achievement of mass salvation and this concept of sacrifice has become a practical and living part of life for the purpose of achieving any goal.

There are three things that I would like to state about sacrifice before progressing. This would ensure that we are on the same platform.

Two Types of Sacrifice

Firstly, there are two types of Sacrifices. We have acceptable sacrifice and unacceptable sacrifice. In other words we have effective and ineffective sacrifices. In the book of Genesis we see two brothers from the same parents and home. The Older one was called Cain and the younger one, Abel. They offered different sacrifices for same purpose and reason and indeed, to the same God. However, Abel's was accepted, but Cain's was not accepted. One of the widely held reasons for the rejection of Cain's sacrifice is the fact that, it was a produce of the cursed ground, which technically, then rendered that sacrifice blemished instead of holy. Furthermore it was below God's expectation of minimum standard. What we would now refer to as 'reasonable'.

I beseech you therefore, brethren, by the mercies of God, that ye present your bodies a living sacrifice, holy, acceptable unto God, which is your reasonable service. (Romans 12:1 Kjv).

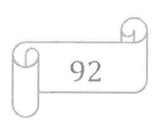

It follows that, the holiness and reasonability of a sacrifice is imperative in qualifying for God's acceptance.

There are various reasons why a sacrifice may or may not be accepted and the opposites are also true. We can safely conclude that an unacceptable sacrifice is a simple waste and the truth of the matter is that, many people particularly Christians are offering wasted sacrifices. May your sacrifice be acceptable in Jesus name!

Secondly, for a sacrifice to be effective, it must meet the expectation of the master or deity to whom or which it is being made. A blessing can only be provoked by a satisfactory sacrifice. Before Isaac released his blessing on Jacob, he requested Esau to bring him venison or savoury food and the key expression and measurement there was 'such as I love'.

And make me savoury food, <u>such as I love</u>, and bring it to me, that I may eat; that my soul may bless you before I die. – Gen 27:4 KJV

It is important to understand that, the sacrifice was not cheap. A sacrifice that does not mean anything or cost the giver, does not move the father and therefore can be classified as *'cheap'*. David, said in 2 Sam 24:24, that he will not sacrifice a burnt offering to God if it does not cost him. When you think about Isaac's request for the venison, it was more or less asking for a costly sacrifice. What do I mean by that?

Time

It could mean the cost of spending a long time and even failed attempts to succeed at hunting the game. No wonder when Jacob delivered the venison Isaac asked him, 'how did you find it so quickly? (Gen 27:20).

It follows that the cost of a sacrifice would not always be in terms of the face value or selling price, but the cost of time invested and injected into it, which may not be obvious by a mere look or assessment of the final product. It is only someone who knows the process involved towards the product that can fully appreciate what is before him or her.

Isaac obviously knew how long it could take and how determined and persistent a person has to be in order to succeed in hunting game.

Blessings are not cheap! If you want to be blessed, you must be ready to sacrifice. If you want to see any change in your circumstance, you would have to make some sacrifices.

Risk

It is quite obvious that hunters themselves are at risk of being hunted. This is because hunting is not done in the open for spectacle but actually done in the territory of other animals which may sometimes include wilder ones like the lions, Cheetahs, leopards etc., who might also be hunting for their own prey. It follows that bringing the venison involved the risking of life and therefore equivalent to blood. Very similar to the water delivered by David's three mighty men in (2 Sam 23:15-16) which David did not drink but poured out before the Lord. This was to say he does not deserve that which only God could be entitled to. The Bible says:

[15] David longed for water and said, "Oh, that someone would get me a drink of water from the well near the gate of Bethlehem!" [16] So the three mighty warriors broke through the Philistine lines, drew water from the well near the gate of Bethlehem and carried it back to David. But he refused to drink it; instead, he poured it out before the LORD.

David was not longing for food, but water. It is a known fact that absence of water or fluid from a man's system is life threatening.

Need of water is similar to need of blood. The Bible says that the life of the flesh is in the blood (Lev 17:11).

The Bible also says concerning Samson in Judges 15:18:

Because he was very thirsty, he cried out to the LORD, "You have given your servant this great victory. Must I now <u>die of thirst</u> and fall into the hands of the uncircumcised?"

It follows that the provision of water to David considering the circumstance was equivalent to blood or life in the sense that:

David had clearly and categorically specified the well from whose water he would drink, he said *'water from the well near the gate of Bethlehem'*. Very similar to Isaac saying *'venison such as I love'*.

Now there could have been many accessible wells, but David knew which particular one he longed for and only from that did he desire to drink. That was his standard measure! *The Well near the gate of Bethlehem* (entrance to the house of bread)

The mighty warriors or men of war might have had to break bounds of the enemy to reach the well. This could have been a process of fighting Philistine guards, risking their own lives etc. in order to draw (not fetch as in our luxury present day from taps) the water.

The well may have been special, well protected and of such good reputation to merit the preference of David. Such wells were usually guarded by large and heavy stones.

Then Jacob went on his journey and came to the land of the people of the east. 2 As he looked, he saw a well in the field, and behold, three flocks of sheep lying beside it, for out of <u>that well</u> the flocks were watered. The stone on the <u>well's mouth was large</u>, 3 and when all the flocks were gathered there, the shepherds would roll the stone from the mouth of the well and water the sheep, and put the stone back in its place over the mouth of the well. (Gen 29:1-3)

These mighty men would have had another task of pushing away the stone to the well before drawing. It was not so simple. Time and energy was invested and sacrificed.

It is also very possible that they did not go with anything with which they could have drawn the water from the well because probably they did not anticipate a situation like this as the whole episode was not the purpose of their journey and the well could have been quite deep too.

"Sir," the woman said, "you have nothing to draw with and the <u>well is deep</u>. Where can you get this living water? JOHN 4:11NIV

So they could well have found a means of drawing either by forcefully taking a pitcher from someone or even possibly borrowing, which would also have rendered them as slaves for that moment. The Bible says:

The rich rule over the poor, and the borrower is <u>slave</u> to the lender. Proverbs 22:7 NIV

All these sacrifices were the price and risks associated with the water David longed for but did not drink in the end. A lot goes in to determine the value of a sacrifice and the value of your sacrifice is the price towards your change you must be willing and ready to pay.

It would be interesting to imagine this happening in our time, risking your life for the head pastor or leader to provide him with a need he has asked or longed for and seeing him or her not using it in the end. Wow, people would be so offended and may even vow 'never again ….'! They may even end up discouraging others from such future assistance to the Pastor.

Likewise the story of the widow's coin! Jesus said she had given all she had to live on. Now, I can deduce from Jesus's statement that, that coin was equivalent to and representative of the widow's blood.

It was her lifeline! If that was all she had to live on, then her life naturally depended on it. She was effectively saying 'I am giving my life as an offering'! There is no bigger offering or sacrifice that can exceed a man's life. Jesus said greater love has no man than this, to lay down His life for his friends (John 15:13). It follows that life is the most precious gift and sacrifice we can ever give and it should only go to God the master changer from whom all blessings flow.

It is unfortunate that many people have erroneously thought that by giving a minimum offering, you are exhibiting humility and emulating the widow and her coin. No! The coin was all this woman had and all she had to live on, so it is more likely that nobody is matching this widows offering at all, even today. Lord increase our faith.

You must protect Your Sacrifice

Thirdly, for a sacrifice to be effective, it must be protected from 'the birds of Prey'. The reason is that, the enemy will always try to attack your sacrifice, your means of fruitfulness and if your means can be destroyed, then your end has technically gone with it. Remember, the thief cometh not but to steal kill and to destroy. In some cases it would even be multiple attempts at different times and occasions. The enemy uses what I would term 'birds of prey', which I deduced from Genesis 15:10-11:

10 Abram brought all these to him, cut them in two and arranged the halves opposite each other; the birds, however, he did not cut in half. 11 <u>Then birds of prey</u> came down on the carcasses, but Abram drove them away.

Here we see a scenario where God was about to enter into a covenant of blessing with Abraham. God had requested a sacrifice which

Abraham had provided. However, the sacrifice came under attack from birds of prey and the Bible says, Abraham drove them away.

There are a lot we can learn from here both on the part of Abraham, representing you and me as believers and the part of our adversary the devil and his agents represented by the birds of Prey.

Don't lose focus

It would be appreciated that, Abraham had kept close watch on his sacrifice. How long before the birds of Prey attacked, we don't exactly know but the fact still remains that he was watching. It could have been hours, but he was watching! It could well have been days, but he was watching. You cannot lose focus, if you want to see your change and breakthroughs come into fruition.

Again, very similar to the scenario of Elijah and Elisha; IF YOU SEE ME GO! How long Elisha, a determined servant to get his blessing had to keep his focus on Elijah, we are not told. This is a clear indication that we don't have to keep only our physical eyes on our sacrifices but also, our spiritual eyes on them. Protecting our sacrifices is our responsibility towards change and fruitfulness, especially through prayer.

It is important to bear in mind that birds of prey can manifest themselves in various ways and not necessarily physically flying birds.

The concept of focus is vital in our walk as Christians towards any form of change and achievement. I personally believe that there are two dimensions of focus. The Visual focus and the Mental focus. Visual focus as the name implies is of the eye whiles the mental is of the mind. It is also fair to say that, they are interlinked and interdependent.

Thou wilt keep him in perfect peace, whose <u>mind</u> is stayed on thee: because he trusteth in thee. Isaiah 26:3 KJV

We can recount the effect of Peter losing focus of Christ and focusing on a boisterous wind. He began to sink. Sinking can be a representation of loss, retrogression and invariably a dance to the drums of the enemy. Now, had Peter not lost focus, he would have become a hero to the glory of God in that aspect.

In order to experience a desired positive change and achievement, the need of focus cannot be over-emphasised. Abraham, Jacob's grandfather was rich. He had his own livestock business and so was his father Isaac. It follows that Jacob was from a lineage of employers but here he was in the house of his uncle Laban, working as an employee with almost nothing to show forth. Jacob had a change he so desired. He wanted to start a family business of his own for his household, as implied in Genesis 30:30. He wanted a unique and unrivalled designer business! Jacob started this business by getting the lambs in his custody to reproduce speckled and spotted lambs. He achieved this by getting the lambs to face or focus on peeled branches during matting and their focus influenced their produce.

Then he placed the peeled branches in all the watering troughs, <u>so that they would be directly in front of the flocks</u> when they came to drink. When the flocks were in heat and came to drink, they mated in front of the branches. And they bore young that were streaked or speckled or spotted. Jacob set apart the young of the flock by themselves, but made the rest face the streaked and dark-colored animals that belonged to Laban. Thus <u>he made separate flocks for himself</u> and did not put them with Laban's animals. Gen 30:37-39 NIV

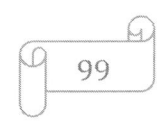

If you can keep your focus on any target be it ministry, education, financial plans or of course marriage, you would realise and reap progressive changes. The act of focus is itself a dimension of sacrifice because there are certain distractions that can be very pleasant and

appealing but you need the discipline to sacrifice that pleasure through your focus.

Birds of Prey Agents

The enemy uses instruments that happen to be available, in order to achieve its aim. One of such instruments is 'people'. There have been many instances where the enemy has used people as birds of prey to attack the sacrifice that would bring about a desired change in another person's life. Changes that would bring them their desired breakthroughs and fulfilment.

As the enemy is crafty and very deceptive, he can use the most unlikely and un-suspected people to strike. Therefore it would be rather erroneous on anybody's part to try and guess a likely person the enemy would use. Furthermore, he takes advantage of a person's qualities and personality and since everybody has their own personality, no one is exempted.

I would like to look at three types of people the enemy uses as birds of prey, although we can appreciate that there are more personalities.

I would like to look at the Absalom, Peter and Judas birds of prey.

The Absalom Birds Of Prey

My terminology of an Absalom bird of prey is that they are so good looking and innocent, it is almost impossible to imagine that they could conceive any form of evil. Their good looks and sometimes innocent face overshadow any form of concealed deception. So as an individual, the better you look, the more careful you should even become and examine yourself daily. Bible says in 2 Sam 14:25 NIV:

In all Israel there was not a man so highly praised for his handsome appearance as Absalom. From the top of his head to the sole of his foot there was no blemish in him.

Absalom birds of prey can be people either in your own family or close circle of friends. No wonder Jesus said in Matt 10:36 that **'a man's foes shall be they of his own household'**.

Why? Because you cannot even suspect. Would you imagine that your own son, brother or sister, would contest and not like to see you successful? But it happens! We can just recall the plot of Joseph's brothers against him. They said *'Come now therefore, and let us slay him, and cast him into some pit, and we will say, some evil beast hath devoured him: and we shall see what will become of his dreams'* (Gen 37:20 KJV). Joseph had no clue of who he was dealing with. You have to rely on the Holy Spirit for help and discernment.

Paul said a great door for effective work has opened to me *and* there are many who oppose me (1Cor 16:9 NIV). The word 'and' rather than 'but' as a conjunction implies that, it is a normal occurrence for opportunities to be attacked and this is one of the reasons why we must be careful.

The Peter Birds Of Prey

I also identify the Peter Birds of Prey. They are the people so spiritual and with divine revelations, it is almost impossible to comprehend that they can be used by the devil as stumbling blocks to attack a sacrifice and to obstruct a person's change.

From that time on Jesus began to explain to his disciples that he must go to Jerusalem and suffer many things at the hands of the elders, chief priests and teachers of the law, and that he must be killed and on the third day be raised to life. Peter took him aside and began to rebuke him. "Never, Lord!" he said. "This shall never happen to you!" Jesus turned and said to Peter, "Get behind me, Satan! You are a stumbling block to me; you do not have in mind the things of God, but the things of men."* Matthew 16:21-23 NIV

How many people would have thought that, the same disciple who caught the revelation of Jesus as the Christ, son of the living God would also be the same instrument of Satan to prevent Jesus from going to the cross as a sacrifice for our sins?

The question is, 'what is the enemy's strategy'? How does he do that? The enemy uses the earthly dimension of wisdom which basically comes across to his victims as a very good and laudable idea, when in actual fact, it is selfish and of a totally un-godly motive (James 3:15). We can probably see best illustration and exposition through the wisdom of Absalom.

The Absalom Wisdom

Absalom won the hearts of the people through earthly wisdom. Like many unfortunate people who have been such instruments of the enemy, Absalom thought he was being smart but it was the devil who had actually out-smarted and enslaved him as a tool for his evil intentions. When you devise any strategy that takes undue advantage of the innocent person, it cannot be wisdom from God and you must shake yourself out of that deception quickly.

After this it happened that Absalom provided himself with chariots and horses, and fifty men to run before him. Now Absalom would rise early and stand beside the way to the gate. So it was, whenever anyone who had a lawsuit came to the king for a decision, that Absalom would call to him and say, "What city are you from?" And he would say, "Your servant is from such and such a tribe of Israel." Then Absalom would say to him, "Look, your case is good and right; but there is no deputy of the king to hear you." Moreover Absalom would say, "Oh, that I were made judge in the land, and everyone who has any suit or cause would come to me; then I would give him justice." And so it was, whenever anyone came near to bow down to him, that he would put out his hand and take him and kiss him. In this manner Absalom acted toward all Israel who came to the king for judgment. So Absalom stole the hearts of the men of Israel. (2 Sam 15:1-6 KJV)

The Absalom 'bird of prey' carefully cultivates an exciting, enticing image. We understand from the scripture that Absalom *got chariots and horses, and fifty men to run before him*. This strategy creates an impression of affluence and sufficiency such that it is impossible to suspect a heart of selfishness and cunningness. *All that glitter is not gold*!

The Absalom strategy involves discipline and hard work. The Bible says Absalom would rise early. This was a discipline adopted not to miss any prey. As the saying goes, "*The early bird catches the worm*." In other words, success comes to those who prepare well and put in an effort. Now, this is a practical principle and therefore works both for the positive and unfortunately for the negative also. Much as this is a strategy to prey on sacrifice and breakthrough, hard work and due diligence helps in realising your desired change manifest.

The Absalom birds of prey know where to position themselves *(beside the way to the gate)*. In Abraham's story, the birds of prey knew exactly where to find the carcass of the sacrifice. Applicably, the Absalom birds of prey know the vantage points to catch their prey and achieve their targets. At the gates where everyone has to pass! Same positioning strategy was adopted by the beggar at the gate of beautiful (Acts 3), a position that could even make his targets feel so guilty to ignore him. Having said that, the element of positioning plays a positive role for a person who likewise needs a positive change.

They look for people who have issues and call them to themselves. (*Anyone who had a lawsuit, Absalom would call to him*) This strategy is rampant in Church these days. Many who are not really working for the Lord but for themselves would sometimes, call people and give them a message that would steal their hearts. Messages that would make people feel that the Absalom bird of prey is on their side, when in reality they are on their personal mission and working in their own selfish interests. This could be a message of complaint against, the church, leaders, managers and supervisors; the same hands that feed and bless them. In some cases they target young, ordinary and innocent members, thereby, causing them to miss their future divine connections and destiny helpers. You have to be careful of people who try to show you faults, omissions and incompetence of your senior pastor and elders. They are dangerous and can obstruct your change.

Absalom took a personal interest in the troubled person and gave them promising, appetising and sympathetic counsel (*What city are you from? your case is good and right*). Absalom birds of prey have an eagle eye, even for troubled people. Every troubled person is potential victim of vulnerability. This is because as they become so desperate, their sense of judgement consequently weakens, causing them to lean towards any form of comfort, regardless of the spirit behind the comfort and its long term disadvantage. The Absalom birds of prey can take advantage of the weak and helpless. Much as we can be vulnerable at one stage or another as human beings, we still need the help of the Holy Spirit to identify and drive away the Absalom birds of prey.

Although Absalom never attacked David directly, he promised the people Justice and who does not like justice? Everyone likes Justice. *'No deputy of the king to hear you Oh, that I were made judge in the land, and everyone who has any suit or cause would come to me; then I would give him justice'.* He gave his prey the impression that their situation could be worse and could only be better if a person of his personality, sympathy and understanding was in charge. In simple terms, the Absolom Birds of prey use the process of emotional manipulation.

Beware of false prophets, which come to you in sheep's clothing, but inwardly they are ravening wolves – Matt 7:15 KJV

The Absalom birds of Prey are in summary like false prophets. Lord Help Us!

The Judas Birds Of Prey

Judas criticised Mary's anointing of Jesus with an expensive nard, advocating that, the perfume could have been sold for an amount which could go a long way in taking care of the poor. That sounds very wise and philanthropic, but was that his true intention?

3 Then Mary took about a pint[a] of pure nard, an expensive perfume; she poured it on Jesus' feet and wiped his feet with her hair. And the house was filled with the fragrance of the perfume.

4 But one of his disciples, Judas Iscariot, who was later to betray him, objected, 5 "Why wasn't this perfume sold and the money given to the poor? It was worth a year's wages.[b]" 6 He did not say this because he cared about the poor but because he was a thief; as keeper of the money bag, he used to help himself to what was put into it. John 12:4-7

Mary's sacrifice was an everlasting memorial because, Jesus himself remarked that she had done a beautiful thing and that wherever the gospel shall be preached her name would be mentioned, but it was initially threatened by the Judas bird of prey which gives an impression that there is a better cause for your sacrifice than the incumbent. So effectively, the Judas bird of prey comes across as if he has the love for the poor at heart when in actual fact he is more interested in his personal comfort and addiction.

Circumstances

We have a personal responsibility to act towards overcoming every trap and deception of the enemy. God told Cain in Genesis 4:7 NIV:

If you do what is right, will you not be accepted? But if you do not do what is right, sin is crouching at your door; it desires to have you, <u>but you must master it</u>."

So the secret is, doing what is right! Failure to do what is right, including managing and respecting the offering which we are presenting to God, rather than treating it with a lackadaisical attitude and neglect, invites sin to crouch at our door.

The good news is that we can and must master it for the bibles says, **'No weapon that is formed against thee shall prosper; and every tongue that shall rise against thee in judgment thou shalt condemn. This is the heritage of the servants of the LORD, and their righteousness is of me, saith the LORD.** Isaiah 54:17 KJV

You must Deal with the Birds Of Prey

In order to see your change come through with regards to your sacrifice, you must deal with the birds of prey. The birds of prey are simply satanic agents that come to frustrate and attack your Sacrifice. They can manifest themselves in various permissible ways.

The Birds of Prey can even attack the Word of God according to Mark 4:4

As he was scattering the seed, some fell along the path, and the birds came and ate it up. Mark 4:4 NIV

In the above scripture Jesus represented the word of God by the seed. By the expression '*the birds came and ate it up*' we are shown the aggression of attack the birds of prey exercise on a seed, which always represents a sacrifice. The aim of the attack is seen in the verse twelve of the chapter as below:

That seeing they may see, and not perceive; and hearing they may hear, and not understand; lest at any time they should be converted, and their sins should be forgiven them. Mark 4:12 KJV

Simply, to obstruct their conversion and salvation. Salvation is the best, biggest and greatest change any human being can ask for and encounter.

Similarly, the serpent in the Garden of Eden attacked the word of God to Adam and to Eve, but he had the permission through the words Eve added to God's word, thereby creating a gap for error. As a result, the devil attacked the mind of Eve by getting her to think she was becoming wiser and exposed to truth. The way to deal with the Birds of prey is in two folds.

The first is not to be ignorant of his schemes.

⁹ Another reason I wrote you was to see if you would stand the test and <u>be obedient in everything</u>. ¹⁰ Anyone you forgive, I also forgive. And what I have forgiven—if there was anything to forgive—I have forgiven in the sight of Christ for your sake,¹¹ in <u>order that Satan might not outwit us</u>. For we are not unaware of his schemes. 2 Cor 2:9-11 NIV

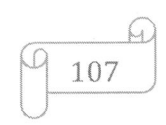

We can safely deduce from the above scripture that, the secret weapon of the enemy is to cause the children of God to fail the test of obedience to God's word and instruction and the most common strategy is to get us to fail the test of forgiving one another.

The second is not to give him any foothold.

In one way or another, every Christian is engaged in a fierce, life-defining battle with Satan. Bible says that 'For we wrestle not against flesh and blood, but against principalities, against powers, against the rulers of the darkness of this world, against spiritual wickedness in high places.' Eph 6:12 KJV.

Satan is our "adversary"(1 Pet 5:8), and he has crafted sumptuous "wiles"(Eph 6:11) and "devices"(2 Cor 2:11) in order to gain ground and win us to his side. In his instruction to dealing with decaying anger, Paul warns us:

"Do not give the devil a foothold". In other words, don't make it any easier for him! This statement teaches us that we must give no ground whatsoever. The smallest ground, the tiniest foothold, the briefest opportunity is to be obsessively guarded against falling into his hand. In this text, unresolved anger that continues to poison our minds and harden our hearts into bitterness and malice give the devil an opening. Scripture admonishes us:

"But put ye on the Lord Jesus Christ, and make not provision for the flesh, to fulfil the lusts thereof "(Rom 13:14 KJV).

Taking the line of sin or warming up to temptation, to see how far you can get, gives ground to the devil and dramatically increases the chances for you to fall into sin. It is imperative not to give the devil even an inch of foothold! If you give him an inch, he will take a yard.

Furthermore, we have power to resist the devil. "Do not give a foothold" emphasizes that this is something within our power and control. The devil can only come as close as we let and allow him. The Bible says "Resist the devil and he will flee from you" (James 4:7).

Though powerful and cunning, the devil can never control our will or force disobedience upon us. Therefore active resistance is of essence! Satan is not one to lay down his arms and take mercy on us out of pity or generosity.

Satan does not go to sleep. He takes no holidays and time offs. Not even a tea break. He is always on the go and on the attack. He only flees from those who have the courage and faith to resist him and turn to God's promise and power. May you turn to God as change makes her way to you, in Jesus name!

CHAPTER 12

IN WHOSE COUNSEL ARE YOU WALKING?

The issue of Counsel plays a very important role in the life of everyone. It was by counsel that the making of mankind was encouraged in Genesis 1:26. 'Then God said, "Let us make mankind in our image, in our likeness, so that they may *rule over* the fish in the sea and the birds in the sky, over the livestock and all the wild animals, and over all the creatures that move along the ground."

So right from the beginning, the issue of Counsel have been very important. It has carried a power of inspiration, co-ordination and then an overall target. In the case of man, the target was to 'rule over'. Now out of love, the book of Psalms starts with one of the most comforting and consoling words anybody would like to hear; '*Blessed*'. It is in the past tense yet, the condition is in the continuous tense.

Blessed is the man that walketh not in the counsel of the ungodly, nor standeth in the way of sinners, nor sitteth in the seat of the scornful.² But his delight is in the law of the LORD; and in his law doth he meditate day and night.

³ And he shall be like a tree planted by the rivers of water, that bringeth forth his fruit in his season; his leaf also shall not wither; and whatsoever he doeth shall prosper. Psalm 1:1-3 KJV

Blessed is the man who 'walketh'. It means that there is a foregone conclusion on the state of a person who does not walk in the counsel of 'the ungodly'.

I wish to establish that a Counsel is also known as advice and also, Counsel is a Spirit. Isaiah 11:2 NIV says,

*The Spirit of the LORD will rest on him— the Spirit of wisdom and of understanding, the **Spirit of counsel** and of might, the Spirit of the knowledge and fear of the LORD—³ and he will delight in the fear of the LORD*

Now, anything that an individual takes into his or her system or body will at one point in time control and direct him or her. If we consider simple water as an example, when we take water into our system eventually we would need to respond to nature's direction of the water in our system. Same goes with strong wine.

Two Types of Counsel

It is fair to say that there are two types of counsel. There is the Counsel of God and the counsel that is not of God; or simply, counsel of the devil. Isaiah 30:1 (AKJV) says:

*Woe to the rebellious children, saith the LORD, that take **counsel, but not of me**; and that cover with a covering, but not of my spirit, that they may add sin to sin:*

It follows that there is a type of counsel that is not of God and such are the counsel that comes from the ungodly.

Un-Godly

It is very easy to assume that the ungodly refers to people who do not believe in God, who do not attend Church or simply, unbelievers.

However, the assessment of a person's godliness is fruit based rather than religion based. A person may be very religious but the fruit they produce does not reflect the goodness in their religion.

The Bible says that no good tree produces evil fruit and no bad tree produces good fruit. (Matt 7:18)

It confirms that every kind of tree is determined by the fruit and described accordingly. A mango tree is called so, because it bears mango as the fruit, not because it looks like one or dwells amongst mango trees. So if a person is godly it would be measured or evidenced by the fruit he or she produces.

Godliness is not measured by how often and punctual a person attends Church. It is not measured by your knowledge and recitation of scriptures but rather measured by your goodness. It is fair to state that goodness is a character of God, as the word 'good' is itself a derivative of God.

Now, a person could be familiar with God and yet be un-godly, based on the fruit he or she produces.

Jesus Christ said,

It's not what goes into your mouth that defiles you; you are defiled by the words that come out of your mouth." Matthew 15:11 NLT

This is a further confirmation that what renders a person ungodly are the words of their mouth as well as their actions and I think this can be a good point for a self-assessment!

Change can be facilitated or obstructed by the counsel you walk in. It is important to have at the back of your mind that, counsel is a spirit. God wants a positive change for you but the counsel and for that matter, the spirit you entertain will determine whether or not you would receive and enjoy the Change on the way to you.

There are various counsels in which people have walked and the consequences must be of valuable warning lessons, for our benefit today. In order to unveil some of these lessons, I wish to discuss just three types of such counsels I have identified. They are: The 'Counsel of Herodias', the 'Counsel of Jonadab' and the Counsel of 'The Ammonite Commanders'.

Counsel of Herodias

(Spirit of Bitterness) – Mark 6:17-29 NIV

17 For Herod himself had given orders to have John arrested, and he had him bound and put in prison. He did this because of Herodias, his Brother Philip's wife, whom he had married. 18 For John had been saying to Herod, "It is not lawful for you to have your brother's wife." 19 So Herodias <u>nursed a grudge</u> against John and wanted to kill him. But she was not able to, 20 because Herod feared John and protected him, knowing him to be a righteous and holy man. When Herod heard John, he was greatly puzzled[c]; yet he liked to listen to him.

21 Finally the opportune time came. On his birthday Herod gave a banquet for his high officials and military commanders and the leading men of Galilee. 22 When the daughter of[d] Herodias came in and danced, she pleased Herod and his dinner guests.

The king said to the girl, "Ask me for anything you want, and I'll give it to you." 23 And he promised her with an oath, "Whatever you ask I will give you, up to half my kingdom."

24 She went out and said to her mother, "What shall I ask for?" "The head of John the Baptist," she answered.

25 At once the girl hurried in to the king with the request: "I want you to give me right now the head of John the Baptist on a platter."

²⁶ *The king was greatly distressed, but because of his oaths and his dinner guests, he did not want to refuse her.* ²⁷ *So he immediately sent an executioner with orders to bring John's head. The man went, beheaded John in the prison,* ²⁸ *and brought back his head on a platter. He presented it to the girl,* **and she gave it to her mother.** ²⁹ *On hearing of this, John's disciples came and took his body and laid it in a tomb.*

The Counsel of Herodias starts with a grudge. As simple and as basic as that. It is usually a grudge borne as a result of a person being victimised for standing up for the truth or enforcing the truth which would have preferably been left unspoken about or even buried.

In the above story, John the Baptist tried to warn Herod of violating the law by marrying his brother's wife. The wife in the person of Herodias then takes a seed of grudge against John because she saw him as an obstacle to her marital destiny and glory.

Herodias as the bible puts it, *'nursed'* the grudge. In other words, she began to feed the grudge, probably by justifying herself as to the validity of the grudge. Probably speaking to herself daily as to what right has John the Baptist to interfere with their private matters etc.? As she probably did this daily, she was effectively watering the seed towards germination and growth. Sometimes we do this without realising the height to which the grudge would grow. Lord help us.

Hebrews 12:15 tells us to look *diligently* lest any man fail of the grace of God, lest any root of bitterness springing up trouble you, and thereby many be defiled.

It means that the effective results of bitterness even affects many people including innocent ones.

As a former wife of Philip, Herodias would not have been an unbeliever. She must have known God. It would be fair to relate her to a present day Christian and therefore could easily be viewed as a 'good tree'. If so, then a good fruit or counsel is her expectant fruit.

The Bible says she nursed a grudge against John and wanted to **kill him**. It follows that the target and desire of the grudge under nursery, was to bring an end to John's life. It means that, unless and until she directly or indirectly kills John, the grudge would still be in nursery without graduating to the target of Herodias.

Victims of Herodias Counsel

The typical victims of Herodias Counsel are people who have great respect for the Herodias of today. People who see others as role models due to their position, qualification, service and even commitment in God's house without a sign that they have anything against anybody.

The daughter of Herodias is a typical example. She had great respect for her mother and trusted in her judgement so much that, she expected the best advice or counsel from her. Therefore given what could probably have been the greatest of opportunities in her life from the King, she wanted to make the best choice. She therefore asked the best person she could think of, the person she deemed loved her more than anybody else, the person she believed had her best interest at heart and probably most mindful of her. Unfortunately she could not see her heart neither could she read her mind!

The King had promised her anything on oath up to half the Kingdom. A pledge which could have changed this girl's life for ever! It's dangerous to have a 'Herodias' in your life. While change is on the way, watch out for 'Herodias'. The question we might ask, is how do we identify a Herodias?

Characteristics of Herodias

Selfishness beyond reason and love. This characteristic does not care about the effect on an individual and the generations after. As a matter of fact, the Herodias Spirit of selfishness is not gender specific and can therefore manifest in anybody including Kings like Hezekiah.

Isaiah 39:5-8 KJV:

⁵ Then said Isaiah to Hezekiah, Hear the word of the L<small>ORD</small> of hosts: ⁶ Behold, the days come, that all that is in thine house, and that which thy fathers have laid up in store until this day, shall be carried to Babylon: nothing shall be left, saith the L<small>ORD</small>. ⁷ And of thy sons that shall issue from thee, which thou shalt beget, shall they take away; and they shall be eunuchs in the palace of the king of Babylon.

⁸ Then said Hezekiah to Isaiah, Good is the word of the L<small>ORD</small> which thou hast spoken. He said moreover, <u>For there shall be peace and truth in my days.</u>

Hezekiah did not care what is taken away, who is taken away, who would be made an eunuch and whatever else, who all these will affect in future, as long as there would be peace in his days. Absolute selfishness!

I would not be wrong in saying that sometimes parents even in this day, have incidentally followed this path, without a second and deeper thought. As a parent myself, I should say 'we must be careful and think more generationally'.

Herodias turned her daughter's opportunity into a selfish privilege of her own, in order to exact her long awaited graduation ceremony of her nursed grudge against John the Baptist, who she could by no other way have reached.

It is very easy to act like Herodias if we don't forgive one another. This can easily happen even in the marital home, where the wife looking for an opportunity to even the score against a husband for one reason or another, will take advantage of the innocent child's opportunity or vice versa. The possibility and instances exists where some wives, probably divorced and bitter, have diverted children's intention from honouring their fathers with gifts, to the errors and sins of their father against them, the mothers. As a result, they have in one way or another, obstructed the children from the promised blessing of long life that comes with honouring a parent. The opposite, where the husband may likewise distort the intention of the children, can also occur to the same effect.

This can also occur in the church. Sometimes, some leaders and gurus who have been in the church for years, highly respected and trusted by the younger ones, might use such opportunities to even their own score with the head Pastor, departmental leads or similar. Therefore if you ever find yourself in a situation upholding retaliation over forgiveness and using someone's opportunity for your implementation, you need to perform a self-diagnostics. There could be a Herodias Spirit somewhere.

Herodias asked her daughter to ask the King for the head of John the Baptist. It is amazing how the girl could not challenge or question her mother's line of decision and suggestion. However, it shows how confident she was in her mother's decision and judgement. She could not judge between the ridicule in her mother's direction from the King's generosity. She did not seem to have engaged any form of personal reasoning whatsoever. Wow, what a level of trust?!

Oh, If only we could have such confidence and trust in God's direction and instruction....?

The girl brings the head of John the Baptist to her mother. Herodias had finally won the desire of her grudge. Probably, you could still hear Herodias punch the air and exclaim, 'Yes!'

Unfortunately, the innocent daughter had lost what could have been a life time blessing of change. She walked in the counsel of the ungodly. The ungodly in this case was her own mother who she saw as good. The ungodly is not a description based on appearance or credibility of status but the fruit produced!

Herodias Counsel will cause you to loose opportunity for territorial increase and coastal expansion. When anybody gives you counsel contrary to your expectation, please remember to ask God. Ideally God should come first.

Trust in the LORD with all thine heart; and lean not unto thine own understanding; In all thy ways acknowledge him, and he shall direct thy paths. – Prov. 3:5 KJV

In Contrast to the counsel of Herodias is the Counsel of Naomi. Naomi gave Ruth, her daughter-in-law or even better described, adopted daughter, a counsel:

*One day Ruth's mother-in-law Naomi said to her, "My daughter, I must find a home[a] for you, where you will be well provided for. ² Now Boaz, with whose women you have worked, is a relative of ours. Tonight he will be winnowing barley on the threshing floor. ³ Wash, put on perfume, and get dressed in your best clothes. Then go down to the threshing floor, but don't let him know you are there until he has finished eating and drinking. ⁴ When he lies down, note the place where he is lying. Then go and uncover his feet and lie down. He will tell you what to do." ⁵ **"I will do whatever you say,"** Ruth answered. ⁶ So she went down to the threshing floor and did everything her mother-in-law told her to do.*

⁷ When Boaz had finished eating and drinking and was in good spirits, he went over to lie down at the far end of the grain pile. Ruth approached quietly, uncovered his feet and lay down. ⁸ In the middle of the night something startled the man; he turned—and there was a woman lying at his feet! ⁹ "Who are you?" he asked.

*"I am your servant Ruth," she said. "Spread the corner of your garment over me, since you are a guardian-redeemer[b] of our family." ¹⁰ "**The Lord bless you, my daughter**," he replied. "This kindness is greater than that which you showed earlier: You have not run after the younger men, whether rich or poor. ¹¹ And now, my daughter, don't be afraid. I **will do for you all you ask**. All the people of my town know that you are a woman of noble character.* Ruth 3:1-11 NIV

This counsel from Naomi to Ruth favourably led to a promise from Boaz to do for Ruth, anything she asks (Ruth 3:11). Through Naomi's counsel the marital vacuum in the life of Ruth was refilled with a wonderful and wealthy replacement in Boaz. This led on to the genealogical arrangement in the *birth* of Jesus Christ, whiles the counsel of Herodias led to the *death* of John the Baptist, the forerunner of Jesus Christ.

In order to see your desired change come to fruition, it's recommendable to follow the counsel of Godly elders and mentors; the 'Naomis of today'; those who have already and successfully walked the paths, with the scars and stars to show, the glories and stories to tell; and like Ruth, do as they advise. Walk in the counsel of 'Naomi' and not of 'Herodias'. You must not miss your change!

Counsel of Jonadab (Spirit of Deception)

There is also the Counsel of Jonadab which is basically a spirit of deception. A terminology I derived from the story of Amnon and Tamar in 2 Samuel 13:1-36 NIV:

In the course of time, Amnon son of David fell in love with Tamar, the beautiful sister of Absalom son of David.² Amnon became so obsessed with his sister Tamar that he made himself ill. She was a virgin, and it seemed impossible for him to do anything to her.³ Now Amnon had <u>an adviser</u> named Jonadab son of Shimeah, David's brother. Jonadab was a very <u>shrewd man</u>. ⁴ He asked Amnon, "Why do you, the king's son, look so haggard morning after morning? Won't you tell me?" Amnon said to him, "I'm in love with Tamar, my brother Absalom's sister."⁵ "Go to bed and pretend to be ill," Jonadab said. "When your father comes to see you, say to him, 'I would like my sister Tamar to come and give me something to eat. Let her prepare the food in my sight so I may watch her and then eat it from her hand.'"

⁶ So Amnon lay down and pretended to be ill. When the king came to see him, Amnon said to him, "I would like my sister Tamar to come and make some special bread in my sight, so I may eat from her hand."⁷ David sent word to Tamar at the palace: "Go to the house of your brother Amnon and prepare some food for him." ⁸ So Tamar went to the house of her brother Amnon, who was lying down. She took some dough, kneaded it, made the bread in his sight and baked it. ⁹ Then she took the pan and served him the bread, but he refused to eat.

"Send everyone out of here," Amnon said. So everyone left him. ¹⁰ Then Amnon said to Tamar, "Bring the food here into my bedroom so I may eat from your hand." And Tamar took the bread she had prepared and brought it to her brother Amnon in his bedroom. ¹¹ But when she took it to him to eat, he grabbed her and said, "Come to bed with me, my sister."

¹² "No, my brother!" she said to him. "Don't force me! Such a thing should not be done in Israel! Don't do this wicked thing. ¹³ What about me? Where could I get rid of my disgrace? And what about you? You would be like one of the wicked fools in Israel. Please speak to the king; he will not keep me from being married to you." ¹⁴ But he refused to listen to her, and since he was stronger than she, he raped her.

¹⁵ Then Amnon hated her with intense hatred. In fact, he hated her more than he had loved her. Amnon said to her, "Get up and get out!"

¹⁶ "No!" she said to him. "Sending me away would be a greater wrong than what you have already done to me."

But he refused to listen to her. ¹⁷ He called his personal servant and said, "Get this woman out of my sight and bolt the door after her." ¹⁸ So his servant put her out and bolted the door after her. She was wearing an ornate[a] robe, for this was the kind of garment the virgin daughters of the king wore. ¹⁹ Tamar put ashes on her head and tore the ornate robe she was wearing. She put her hands on her head and went away, weeping aloud as she went.

²⁰ Her brother Absalom said to her, "Has that Amnon, your brother, been with you? Be quiet for now, my sister; he is your brother. Don't take this thing to heart." And Tamar lived in her brother Absalom's house, a desolate woman.

²¹ When King David heard all this, he was furious. ²² And Absalom never said a word to Amnon, either good or bad; he hated Amnon because he had disgraced his sister Tamar.

²³ Two years later, when Absalom's sheepshearers were at Baal Hazor near the border of Ephraim, he invited all the king's sons to come there. ²⁴ Absalom went to the king and said, "Your servant has had shearers come. Will the king and his attendants please join me?"

²⁵ "No, my son," the king replied. "All of us should not go; we would only be a burden to you." Although Absalom urged him, he still refused to go but gave him his blessing.

²⁶ Then Absalom said, "If not, please let my brother Amnon come with us."

The king asked him, "Why should he go with you?" ²⁷ But Absalom urged him, so he sent with him Amnon and the rest of the king's sons.

²⁸ Absalom ordered his men, "Listen! When Amnon is in high spirits from drinking wine and I say to you, 'Strike Amnon down,' then kill him. Don't be afraid. Haven't I given you this order? Be strong and brave." ²⁹ So Absalom's men did to Amnon what Absalom had ordered. Then all the king's sons got up, mounted their mules and fled.

³⁰ While they were on their way, the report came to David: "Absalom has struck down all the king's sons; not one of them is left." ³¹ The king stood up, tore his clothes and lay down on the ground; and all his attendants stood by with their clothes torn.

³² But Jonadab son of Shimeah, David's brother, said, "My lord should not think that they killed all the princes; only Amnon is dead. This has been Absalom's express intention ever since the day Amnon raped his sister Tamar. ³³ My lord the king should not be concerned about the report that all the king's sons are dead. **Only Amnon is dead.**"

³⁴ Meanwhile, Absalom had fled.

Now the man standing watch looked up and saw many people on the road west of him, coming down the side of the hill. The watchman went and told the king, "I see men in the direction of Horonaim, on the side of the hill."[b]

³⁵ Jonadab said to the king, "See, the king's sons have come; it has happened just as your servant said."

36 *As he finished speaking, the king's sons came in, wailing loudly. The king, too, and all his attendants wept very bitterly.*

Amnon was the very first son of King David and therefore under normal human law and monarchical arrangement, would have been destined for the throne of David. However, a spirit of deception was sown into him via a counsel I call the *counsel of Jonadab*.

From the Scripture above of the verse 3, we gather that Amnon had an adviser called Jonadab. This gives me an impression that the counsel concerning Tamar is not the only one he might have ever given Amnon to merit the title of an 'adviser'. It would seem to me that Jonadab had probably given Amnon a few counsels before. However, the details and result of those counsels are not given.

Probably they were counsels that resulted in the direction and expectation of Amnon and for that reason, he had given Jonadab his desired credibility. Thenceforth, Amnon would have had no reason to doubt and critically examine Jonadab's advice any more. Jonadab had become a credible adviser.

He was his Cousin

By way of Jonadab being a cousin of Amnon, the latter might have trusted Jonadab's advice to be out of love, and blood relation that, it could not be wrong. Furthermore, Tamar was not a foreigner either. She was related to both.

This is clearly one of the strategies and gates of the enemy. He uses those close and related to you in order that, you might lose any sense of suspicion. We saw this in Herodias, as well as Judas Iscariot. Judas ate from the same bowl with Jesus but was still a vessel of the enemy.

And a man's foes shall be they of his own household. Matt 10:36 KJV

He was very shrewd

The character of Jonadab described as very Shrewd in the same verse 3, is an indication of a typical aptitude that sums it all up. It simply means, 'that is how he is' and a derivative character of the Snake which is deception and robbery or earthly wisdom.

16 'I am sending you out like sheep among wolves. Therefore be as shrewd as snakes and as innocent as doves. – Matt 10:16 NIV

One of the major effects of the Counsel of Jonabad is that, it can rob you of your inheritance. As a result of this counsel not only did Amnon lose his opportunity to inherit the throne of David, he also lost his life. Similarly, the counsel of the serpent robbed Eve and Adam of their inherited garden and also their Spiritual life.

Do not allow 'Jonadab' to obstruct your change for elevation God is bringing!

A Jonadab Spirit does not care nor value your life. The scripture in verse 33 says 'My lord the king should not be concerned about the report that all the king's sons are dead. **Only Amnon is dead.**'

This was just like Jonadab saying, the loss of Amnon's life is not such a big deal to lament over and accordingly, he showed no sympathetic emotion nor remorse. He was able to finish his speech in piece but only to see the King himself and his sons all weeping at the end. The Bible says:

36 As he finished speaking, the king's sons came in, wailing loudly. The king, too, and all his attendants wept very bitterly.

The Jonadab Counsel leaves a good and happy home sorrowful. Change is on the way, but you must watch out for the Jonadabs in the family and let's also watch out for the Jonadabs even in our Churches. You must not miss your change!

Jonadab or Jonathan?

In contrast to the counsel of Jonadab is what I term, 'the counsel of Jonathan'. Jonadab was the friend of Amnon and Jonathan the son of Saul, was the friend of David. The counsel of Jonadab was of deception, the counsel of Jonathan was of protection.

Saul told his son Jonathan and all the attendants to kill David. But Jonathan had taken a great liking to David ² and warned him, "My father Saul is looking for a chance to kill you. Be on your guard tomorrow morning; go into hiding and stay there. ³ I will go out and stand with my father in the field where you are. I'll speak to him about you and will tell you what I find out." – 1 Sam 19:1-3 NIV.

Amnon walked in the counsel of Jonadab, it led him to his death. David on the other hand, walked in the counsel of Jonathan, he escaped the plot of his death. Two counsels, two extremes!

You may not have the ability of choosing your siblings but you do have the ability of choosing your friends. Change is on the way but who you choose as a friend could determine whether you miss or meet your change. 'Jonadab' or 'Jonathan'? I would suggest, you go for 'Jonathan'!

Counsel of the Ammonite Commanders

(Assumption)

Finally, counsel of the Ammonite Commanders. This is basically the spirit of assumption.

In the course of time, Nahash king of the Ammonites died, and his son succeeded him as king. 2 David thought, 'I will show kindness to Hanun son of Nahash, because his father showed kindness to me.' So David sent a delegation to express his sympathy to Hanun concerning his father.

When David's envoys came to Hanun in the land of the Ammonites to express sympathy to him, 3 the Ammonite commanders said to Hanun, 'Do you think David is honouring your father by sending envoys to you to express sympathy? Haven't his envoys come to you only to explore and spy out the country and overthrow it?' 4 So Hanun seized David's envoys, shaved them, cut off their garments at the buttocks, and sent them away.

5 When someone came and told David about the men, he sent messengers to meet them, for they were greatly humiliated. The king said, 'Stay at Jericho till your beards have grown, and then come back.' 6 When the Ammonites realised that they had become obnoxious to David, Hanun and the Ammonites sent a thousand talents[a] of silver to hire chariots and charioteers from Aram Naharaim,[b] Aram Maakah and Zobah. 7 They hired thirty-two thousand chariots and charioteers, as well as the king of Maakah with his troops, who came and camped near Medeba, while the Ammonites were mustered from their towns and moved out for battle. - Chronicles 19:1-7 NIV

David had thought of reciprocating the kindness of Nahash to his son Hanun and for that reason, had sent a delegation to express that gesture to Hanun.

The Commanders of Ammon however diverted the expectation and reception of Hanun through their Counsel. They got Hanun to look at David's gesture from an angle, totally contrary and opposite to the theme of David's order for his Envoys. The Ammonite Commanders had assumed that, David's envoys had come to spy and overthrow their land. Now, any King will rise and raise his highest defence against a plot like that.

King Hanun reacts to this counsel which was birthed out of assumption, by seizing David's Envoys, Shaving off their hair and humiliating them in such an awful way as cutting their garments at their buttocks. This was a deliberate act that reduced and degraded innocent grown up men, aside disrespecting their religion and probable covenantal obligations to their God, by not shaving off the hairs on their heads. The ridicule and mockery aspect engineered by the slit buttocks of their garments is beyond imagination.

The godly give good advice to their friends; the wicked lead them astray. Proverbs 12:26 (NLT)

Friends and Allies

When you walk in the counsel of negative assumption, you lose potentially valuable friends and allies. Can you imagine having David as a friend and ally? Unfortunately Hanun missed this benefit because he believed in a counsel born out of shear assumption. He could have become a friend and an ally of King David the warrior. Unfortunately, every other possible benefit of that good friendship with David went out of the window. It is good to have and know a person's history. However, it can also be erroneous when the information is archaic and the person has either changed, or you happen to be the one who is rather uninformed about the true circumstances surrounding what you know. What we all need is wisdom. Bibles says 'wisdom is the principal thing, so get wisdom, but in all your getting, get understanding.

Unnecessary Expense

We realise from the scripture that, the ammonites spent money in hiring chariots and charioteers in preparation to fight and defend themselves against David. This was an expenditure that should not have occurred but it did because, somebody produced a fruit of false assumption. It follows that when you walk in the counsel of the ungodly, you can incur unnecessary expenditure. You could end up spending money in defence from non-existent threats and enemies; enemies that only exist in your mind through a transfer from the 'Ammonite commanders'. Don't allow somebody's assumption to create enemies in your mind to adversely affect your financial status!

Scripture advices as follows:

Be careful for nothing; but in everything by prayer and supplication with thanksgiving let your requests be made known unto God. And the peace of God, which passeth all understanding, shall keep your hearts and minds through Christ Jesus. Phil 4:6-7 KJV

CHAPTER 13
LOOSED CHANGE

God wants to see His children delivered from every form of oppression and captivity. The boy born blind in our primary scripture was in captivity and deprivation of sight but by the redemptive power of God he was loosed from that bondage and released into evangelistic mission. God wants to bring you the change of total release into total fulfilment. Unless you become totally freed from all restrictions, there is still a need that God wants to meet because He is the specialist for such appointments. The Story of Lazarus is one of the most beautiful, lessons packed, grace, deliverance and power of God messages I love and as we explore it together, I believe we can be assured that change is indeed on the way.

John 11 - King James Version (KJV)

11 Now a certain man was sick, named Lazarus, of Bethany, the town of Mary and her sister Martha.² (It was that Mary which anointed the Lord with ointment, and wiped his feet with her hair, whose brother Lazarus was sick.) ³ Therefore his sisters sent unto him, saying, Lord, behold, he whom thou lovest is sick.

⁴ When Jesus heard that, he said, this sickness is not unto death, but for the glory of God, that the Son of God might be glorified thereby.⁵ Now Jesus loved Martha, and her sister, and Lazarus.⁶ When he had heard therefore that he was sick, he abode two days still in the same place where he was.

⁷ Then after that saith he to his disciples, Let us go into Judaea again. ⁸ His disciples say unto him, Master, the Jews of late sought to stone thee; and goest thou thither again?

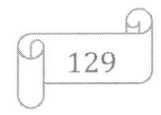

⁹ Jesus answered, Are there not twelve hours in the day? If any man walk in the day, he stumbleth not, because he seeth the light of this world. ¹⁰ But if a man walk in the night, he stumbleth, because there is no light in him.

¹¹ These things said he: and after that he saith unto them, our friend Lazarus sleepeth; but I go, that I may awake him out of sleep. ¹² Then said his disciples, Lord, if he sleep, he shall do well. ¹³ Howbeit Jesus spake of his death: but they thought that he had spoken of taking of rest in sleep. ¹⁴ Then said Jesus unto them plainly, Lazarus is dead.

¹⁵ And I am glad for your sakes that I was not there, to the intent ye may believe; nevertheless let us go unto him. ¹⁶ Then said Thomas, which is called Didymus, unto his fellow disciples, Let us also go, that we may die with him. ¹⁷ Then when Jesus came, he found that he had lain in the grave four days already. ¹⁸ Now Bethany was nigh unto Jerusalem, about fifteen furlongs off:

¹⁹ And many of the Jews came to Martha and Mary, to comfort them concerning their brother. ²⁰ Then Martha, as soon as she heard that Jesus was coming, went and met him: but Mary sat still in the house. ²¹ Then said Martha unto Jesus, Lord, if thou hadst been here, my brother had not died. ²² But I know, that even now, whatsoever thou wilt ask of God, God will give it thee. ²³ Jesus saith unto her, Thy brother shall rise again. ²⁴ Martha saith unto him, I know that he shall rise again in the resurrection at the last day. ²⁵ Jesus said unto her, I am the resurrection, and the life: he that believeth in me, though he were dead, yet shall he live:

²⁶ And whosoever liveth and believeth in me shall never die. Believest thou this? ²⁷ She saith unto him, Yea, Lord: I believe that thou art the Christ, the Son of God, which should come into the world.

²⁸ And when she had so said, she went her way, and called Mary her sister secretly, saying, The Master is come, and calleth for thee. ²⁹ As soon as she heard that, she arose quickly, and came unto him. ³⁰ Now

Jesus was not yet come into the town, but was in that place where Martha met him. ³¹ The Jews then which were with her in the house, and comforted her, when they saw Mary, that she rose up hastily and went out, followed her, saying, She goeth unto the grave to weep there.

³² Then when Mary was come where Jesus was, and saw him, she fell down at his feet, saying unto him, Lord, if thou hadst been here, my brother had not died. ³³ When Jesus therefore saw her weeping, and the Jews also weeping which came with her, he groaned in the spirit, and was troubled.

³⁴ And said, where have ye laid him? They said unto him, Lord, come and see.

³⁵ Jesus wept.

³⁶ Then said the Jews, Behold how he loved him! ³⁷ And some of them said, Could not this man, which opened the eyes of the blind, have caused that even this man should not have died? ³⁸ Jesus therefore again groaning in himself cometh to the grave. It was a cave, and a stone lay upon it.

³⁹ Jesus said, Take ye away the stone. Martha, the sister of him that was dead, saith unto him, Lord, by this time he stinketh: for he hath been dead four days. ⁴⁰ Jesus saith unto her, Said I not unto thee, that, if thou wouldest believe, thou shouldest see the glory of God? ⁴¹ Then they took away the stone from the place where the dead was laid. And Jesus lifted up his eyes, and said, Father, I thank thee that thou hast heard me.

⁴² And I knew that thou hearest me always: but because of the people which stand by I said it, that they may believe that thou hast sent me. ⁴³ And when he thus had spoken, he cried with a loud voice, Lazarus, come forth. ⁴⁴ And he that was dead came forth, bound hand and foot with graveclothes: and his face was bound about with a napkin. Jesus saith unto them, loose him, and let him go.

⁴⁵ Then many of the Jews which came to Mary, and had seen the things which Jesus did, believed on him. ⁴⁶ But some of them went their ways to the Pharisees, and told them what things Jesus had done.

⁴⁷ Then gathered the chief priests and the Pharisees a council, and said, what do we? For this man doeth many miracles.

Delays are not denials

This great story is a clear demonstration of Jesus' supremacy over all things and testifies that as far as God is concerned, delays are not denials and nothing is ever too late with God. Change is on the way!

The first fascinating thing in this passage is the identity of the man who was sick and eventually died. He was Lazarus of Bethany, the brother of Martha and Mary and much more, the "one Jesus loved". Now, the question I ask myself is this: How come Jesus' friend fell sick? As part of life today, I am sure we all ask very similar questions when we discover people we deem so committed to God, going through sufferings, inflictions and afflictions.

As you read, you might probably be going through an issue in one way or another and might have even been wondering about the reason why you are going through that. Consequently you might have been asking yourself whether God truly loves you, if he has allowed that situation to plaque you so much. Well, this account from John 11 settles the issue. In the Bible, the one Jesus loved became sick to the point of death but since the God of love and miracles is not dead, he will change your situation also, in Jesus name! Bible says:

Many are the afflictions of the righteous: but the LORD delivereth him out of them all. Psalm 34:19 KJV

Another unusual thing was Jesus's response to the emergency call, sent to him about the sickness of Lazarus his friend. When he was told, He said, this sickness *is not unto* death but rather unto the glory of God. In other words, the sickness is not to the credit and glory of the power of death, but rather to bring glory and honour unto Jehovah God. Hallelujah! Quite similar to that of the boy born blind in our background story.

Now, as Christians this is the kind of stance we should take when confronted with issues like this. Unfortunately some of us rather give up earlier than the sick person himself or herself and even prophesy credit and power to death, thereby eliminating the power of God out of the picture entirely. Lord help us!

The Bible says, Jesus stayed two more days where he was. One would have expected him to get up and rush off to Bethany on hearing the news about His friend but he did not. *Someone, might ask, 'friends like these who needs enemies..?'*

Similarly, there are certain things you might have urgently placed before God but it seems God is delaying. As a matter of fact, sometimes we describe a situation as delayed when in actual fact, we are the ones who are either in a hurry ahead of ourselves or simply impatient. One thing you need to understand is that every seemingly delayed situation in your life may be for a purpose, and every purpose of God is based on His timing rather than man's timing.

As you may recall from earlier readings, Jesus did not run into producing wine simply because of circumstantial time but based on heaven's time for him. He said *'my time has not yet come'*. Jesus knew and appreciated divine timing. In God's time, all the jigsaws come together. That is when the beauty in the mess comes to present her message. Hallelujah!

He has made everything beautiful in its time: also he has put eternity in men's hearts, so that no man can find out the work that God does from the beginning to the end. Eccl 3:11 KJV

Lazarus died and he was abandoned to the grave by those who loved him. There was nothing further they could do. They could not go to the grave with him. There are limits to how far relatives can go with you. It's only Jesus who can go anywhere with you at any time and indeed, in any situation. As a matter of fact it is only God who can send you and yet, accompany you at the same time. God sent Moses to Egypt and accompanied him by His presence.

Never too late

When Jesus got there he was told, not to go near the grave because by then Lazarus was stinking! In other words, he had gone beyond the point of rescue and salvage. Everyone concluded that it was too late and it was all over. It is possible that, some people you love and also love you or at least claim to love you have come to the same conclusion about you in one way or another. I can guess that people had their conclusion regarding Sarah and Abraham, Elizabeth and Zechariah. May be like Zechariah the priest, you have been dedicating other people's babies as a Pastor, praying for others towards the fruits of their wombs and hearing their consequent testimonies but you are still believing God for your own breakthrough. However, as you read this book, I wish to encourage you that, the same page on which people and society have written their conclusion, shall be the same page on which the God of change will write His introduction about you! By His mighty and miraculous hand people will hear your testimony and when they do, they will sponsor you to travel round and share it, in Jesus name!

Anyway, Jesus went to the entrance of the grave and the only perfect high priest who can be touched with the feeling of our infirmities wept because of Lazarus despite the fact that he knew Lazarus will live again. Your dreams and aspirations can also live again, because change is on the way!

Roll Away Limitation

Jesus ordered that the stone at the entrance be rolled away. Every stone hindering your breakthrough must give way at the sight of Jesus. It is worth noting that, Jesus did not roll away the stone but he commanded the people around and watching, to do that. I believe that Jesus took this line of action for two reasons:

Firstly, because he was not responsible for placing the stone on the tomb. Therefore the people responsible should be the same people to remove that hindrance. In the book of Daniel Chapter 6:16 NIV, it was king Darius who ordered Daniel to be thrown into the lion's Den and he was the same person who interceded in prayer for him saying, 'May your God whom you serve continually rescue you'. By the authority of the Holy Ghost, any enemy real or fake that might be causing you undue hindrance and limitation, whether physically or spiritually, will reverse their actions in Jesus name!

Secondly, God will not do what he has mandated and capacitated man to do. He shares his glory with no man, therefore he specialises in the impossible so man can carry out the possible. He brings within the reach of man, what man cannot achieve naturally but does not usually go beyond. He always gets man to do what man is capable of. The story about the axe head in 2 Kings 6, elucidates this:

5 But as one was felling a beam, the axe head fell into the water; and he cried out and said, "Alas, my master! For it was borrowed." 6 Then the man of God said, "Where did it fall?" And when he showed him the *place, he cut off a stick, and threw it in there, and made the iron float. 7 And he said, "<u>Take it up for yourself.</u>" So he put out his hand and took it.* 2 Kings 6:5-7   NASB

The man of God miraculously enabled the axe head to float, but he did not progress any further to picking it up for the servant but asked him to take it up for himself. Similarly God brings certain changes our way but we have to play our role to actually experience and benefit from its provision.

Call Forth

Jesus cried out to Lazarus 'come forth'! By the authority in the name of Jesus, you have the mandate to call forth any kind of Lazarus in your life. Your Lazarus can be anything or entitlement that has been buried in one way or another, hindered from your reach in one way or another and by the power in Jesus name you must call it forth.

[9] Wherefore God also hath highly exalted him, and given him a name which is above every name: [10] That at the name of Jesus every knee should bow, of things in heaven, and things in earth, and things under the earth; - Phil 2:9-10

When death which had held Lazarus, heard the voice of Jesus, it gave him up instantly. Every evil power holding you or your property captive will give you up to enter into your blessings and destiny fulfilment in the name of Jesus!

Now the man who had been dead for four days got up! I declare and speak forth the power and spirit of God that raised Christ from the dead, to enter and enable you to get up and out of anything that has kept you or your family down right now, in Jesus name! Your change is on the way!

CHAPTER 14

TOTAL FREEDOM

(bound hand and foot with graveclothes: and his face was bound about with a napkin)

The story of Lazarus is apart from all, packed with interesting lessons for us as human beings and particularly Christians. It is very easy to question the love of the Lord for us when faced with certain situations. However from the story we can comfortably say, until God says it's over, it cannot be over. There are three main areas that the scripture categorically indicated that Lazarus was bound. The hands, face and feet and these were the specifics where he had to be unbound for total freedom. It may seem simple in general and on the surface but there are deeper implications, on which I would like to elucidate.

Hands Loosed for Blessing

The bound hands could represent restriction from work, savings and investment. The Bible says God will bless the works of thy hand.

Seven days shalt thou keep a solemn feast unto the LORD thy God in the place which the LORD shall choose: because the LORD thy God shall bless thee in all thine increase, and in **all the works of thine hands**, *therefore thou shalt surely rejoice – Deut 16:15 KJV*

So if the hands are bound, it means they cannot work and invariably they would have nothing to bless.

Economically, this would affect income generation which would reduce the marginal propensity to savings and investment and then lead to a vicious cycle of poverty. So being bound of the hands is effectively a spiritual means of the enemy keeping a person in the bondage of poverty. So considering the situation of Lazarus, he was out of the grave but still bound in poverty from unemployment. However, Jesus said loose him and let him go. It means be loosed from the captivity of poverty and go. Go where? Go into the freedom of financial abundance. We must be ready to work with our hands as the scripture says:

You will eat the fruit of your labor; blessings and prosperity will be yours – Psalm 128:2 NIV

As your hands become loose, may contracts and employments chase you! In the book of 2 Kings 6:6-7 we realised that, although Elisha miraculously enabled the axe head to float, the servant needed a free hand to reach out and take it. A bound hand cannot take what God miraculously avails for easy possession. It means that unless and until hands are freed spiritually and even physically, one could be surrounded by Godly opportunities but would not be able to take them. May your hands be loosed and loosed more, in Jesus name!

Hands Loosed for Foundations

With the hands foundations are laid. The bible says:

The hands of Zerubbabel have laid the foundation of this house; his hands shall also finish it; and thou shalt know that the LORD of hosts hath sent me unto you. Zech 4:9 KJV

The scripture confirms that foundations are laid by the hands and completion is also by the same hands. It follows that unless the hands are loosed, one can be alive but unfortunately, cannot start nor finish any project. There are people who for some reason have never been able to complete anything they start. They either get discouraged along the way or simply quit out of laziness, lack of endurance and perseverance and that has become the norm and cycle. It follows that discouragement, laziness and pure careless lifestyle can be forms of grave bandages or clothes that need to come off. It is not always an act of the devil to experience bound hands. Sometimes, it can be a personal preference and a personal choice. There are some people, even if you bring a Job application form to them, you would also have to beg them to complete it and even make it your own responsibility to post the forms to the companies or deliver it for them. Laziness and careless lifestyles are grave clothes. They must be loosed for the coming change.

As you read this book, you shall declare saying, in the name of Jesus, any project that my hands shall start, my hands will also finish. For by the redemptive power in the blood of Jesus, I cannot be limited. I am loose from every bandage on my hands and I shall be a living testimony unto God!

Hands for War

Blessed be the LORD my strength, who teaches my hands to war, and my fingers to fight: Psalm 144:1 KJV

The Bible says that we do not fight against flesh and blood, but with forces and principalities and against the rulers of darkness. It simply means that there is a spiritual war in which every Christian is without a choice, engaged. Now David records as a testimony that, it is God who strengthens by teaching, controlling and supporting his hands in war from fatigue. It follows that your hands have to be free, available and co-operative for God to use them. They must be loosed and not bound. The battle between the Israelites and Amalekites (Exodus 17) was won through free lifted hands of prayer. The Staff of God was lifted in the free hands of Moses. Moses's hands were also supported by the free hands of Aaron and Hur. I believe these two men were not there accidentally but God was presenting a message by their lineage. Aaron's hand represented intercessory prayer since he stood for the priestly line of Levi, whiles that of Hur represented Praise as he was from the lineage of Judah. We can therefore infer that victory was wrought through the power of Prayer and Praise. This can be further and more beautifully supported by the Story of Paul and Silas in Jail (Acts 16). The Bible says, they prayed and sang hymns and suddenly there was such a violent earthquake that the foundations of the prison were shaken and at once all the prison doors flew open, and everyone's chains came loose. What a Victory, what a change?! It all started with free hands. Your change is also on the way and as you lift up your free hands of prayer and praise, every spiritual prison foundation in your life or that of your family or anybody connected to you, will be shaken for total freedom in Jesus name!

Lift up your hands in the sanctuary and praise the LORD – Psalm 134:2 NIV

If you can keep your hands lifted in Praise, it would be too hot for the enemy to bind and restrict.

Bound Feet

Significance and effects of Bound feet

When your feet are bound you can only hop but not walk nor run. It follows that you cannot go far neither can you progress up to standard, let alone above standard.

However, it is God who makes your feet like hinds feet and enables you to walk in your high places.

The LORD God is my strength, and he will make my feet like hinds' feet, and he will make me to walk upon <u>mine high places.</u> To the chief singer on my stringed instruments. - Habakkuk 3:19 KJV

So when your feet are bound you automatically miss the ability to walk in high places. It means that you are unable to reach places of promotion and prominence. When promotion keeps eluding you, your feet might have been spiritually bound but may your feet be loosed and freed to take your place of promotion and elevation, in Jesus name.

I particularly like the expression 'mine high places'. It means that there are certain high places that specially and specifically belong to you! As change makes its way to you, may the Lord God be your strength and may He grant you divine enablement to walk in your allotted high place and take your entitled seat of promotion and establishment in Jesus name.

Secondly when feet are bound, you cannot run. Which means speed is deprived and retarded. Under such a condition, you may find it hard to catch up and almost impossible to overtake. However, as you carry on reading, by the supreme power of the Holy Ghost, I command whatever might have restricted your mobility in one way or another to lose you now and let you go!

The power of the LORD came on Elijah and, tucking his cloak into his belt, he ran ahead of Ahab all the way to Jezreel. – 1 Kings 18:46

May the power of God come upon you to operate in the anointing for divine acceleration and overtaking! May you recover all that you had missed and all that you had lost, in Jesus name!

I must state and explain that every form of acceleration comes with risks that must be managed and possibly avoided.

The scripture above implies that before Elijah ran ahead, he tucked his cloak into his belt. What this simply means is that, Elijah dealt with any possible risk of entanglement in the process, which could have caused him destruction, loss of balance and eventually, a fall.

A similar method of risk management was exercised by Blind man Bartimaeus in Mark 10:46-52. When Jesus called Bartimaeus over, He threw away his coat, his garment which was probably his only possession, but could also have caused him to stumble on his way to reaching Jesus. He was ready to get rid of anything that could obstruct him on his way. In simple terms you could benefit from the authoritative power of God for a change by divine speed but you have a personal responsibility to ensure that you are adequately prepared otherwise the result could be rather shorter than your expectation.

It's very easy to admire the strategy and accuracy of David in killing Goliath with the sling and a stone. However, not much is known as to how long he had been practicing with the sling for, nor the difficult circumstances, the fire and miss here and there, but God knew his preparation and therefore was ready to back him. May God back you also, even as you prepare to embrace your change on the way, in Jesus name!

The process of tucking in the cloak or girding up your loins could be in the form of giving up the old garment of self-pity or self-righteousness, taking up a course to upgrade yourself and skills etc.

When I came to the UK, I met some friends who were here before I arrived but were not interested in furthering their education in order to upgrade themselves and prepare for better job opportunities that existed. However, I managed to do differently. As a result and by the grace of God, I happened to achieve more in a shorter time compared to them. I was prepared. I had tucked in my cloak. I tucked in my cloak through selective friendship and counsel. I had to side-line and side step those who were not ambitious, out of my life and draw-in those whose life and style challenged me to go up higher. Sometimes, we shy away from colleagues whose success expose our failures and short-falls but if we actually tackle it differently, it would help us in the end. The Bible says in Proverbs 13:20 that, he who walks with the wise shall be wise but a companion of fools shall be destroyed.

Unlike any of his brothers, Eliab, Abinadab, Shimeah etc. David was prepared as a Shepherd boy; a task he executed with passion in the wilderness and that, coupled with the power of God that came upon him by anointing, guaranteed that he would excel and exceed expectation in the palace. Your wilderness could be your place of preparation and opportunity to tuck in your cloak, ready for the speed and progress to your destiny. Change is on the way!

I believe the reason why God does not always grant us certain breakthroughs is not due to the absence of His power but rather our lack of adequate preparation to accommodate the change. God is unlikely to bless you with what you will misuse and effectively abuse, due to inadequate preparation and appreciation.

One of the ways by which you tuck in your cloak in order to avoid entanglement on your Journey to the top is by leaving certain companions. Sometimes this can be a hard choice and route to take but it has to be done. The potential effect of wrong companionship as a form of bound feet from promotion or elevation is well illustrated in 2 Kings 9; a story about Jehu, I would like us to explore and expose. Again, as a kind of subroutine, before progressing with other effects of bound feet:

The prophet Elisha summoned a man from the company of the prophets and said to him, "Tuck your cloak into your belt, take this flask of olive oil with you and go to Ramoth Gilead. ² When you get there, look for Jehu son of Jehoshaphat, the son of Nimshi. Go to him, <u>get him away from his companions</u> and take him into an inner room. ³ Then take the flask and pour the oil on his head and declare, 'This is what the LORD says: I anoint you king over Israel.' Then open the door and run; don't delay!"

4 *So the young prophet went to Ramoth Gilead.* **5** *When he arrived, he found the <u>army officers sitting together</u>. "I have a message for you, <u>commander</u>," he said. <u>"For which of us</u>?" asked Jehu. "For you, commander," he replied.*

He found the army officers sitting together. It means that they were of the same rank. However by asking, the young prophet managed to identify Jehu and directed his message to him accordingly without necessarily mentioning his name. Hence Jehu asking 'which of us'…….

6 *Jehu got up and went into the house. Then the prophet poured the oil on Jehu's head and declared, "This is what the* Lord*, the God of Israel, says: 'I anoint you king over the* Lord*'s people Israel.* **7** *You are to destroy the house of Ahab your master, and I will avenge the blood of my servants the prophets and the blood of all the* Lord*'s servants shed by Jezebel.* **8** *The whole house of Ahab will perish. I will cut off from Ahab every last male in Israel—slave or free.*[a] **9** *I will make the house of Ahab like the house of Jeroboam son of Nebat and like the house of Baasha son of Ahijah.* **10** *As for Jezebel, dogs will devour her on the plot of ground at Jezreel, and no one will bury her.'" Then he opened the door and ran.* **11** *When Jehu went out to his fellow officers, one of them asked him, "Is everything all right? Why did this maniac come to you?"*

"You know the man and the sort of things he says," Jehu replied. **12** *"That's not true!" they said. "Tell us."*

Jehu said, "Here is what he told me: 'this is what the Lord *says: I anoint you king over Israel.'"* **13** *They quickly took their cloaks and spread them under him on the bare steps. Then they blew the trumpet and shouted, "Jehu is king!"*

God knew who he wanted to bless and knew exactly where he was located. He was located in Ramoth Gilead so he sent his instrument or messenger of blessing to the exact location. The blessing of God shall locate you also, at your very position and point of need.

He was specific on whom he was looking to bless. The scripture said 'look for Jehu, the son of Jehoshaphat, the son of Nimshi'. In a similar description, you are marked and chosen for a blessing however, you need to spot the signs and characteristics of obstructive companions.

Obstructive Companions Defame

11 *When Jehu went out to his fellow officers, one of them asked him, "Is everything all right? Why did this <u>maniac</u> come to you?"*

From the scripture, you realise that the companions had no respect for the messenger of Elisha and had branded him a *maniac.*

If you find yourself in the midst of people who have no respect for people you respect example, your Pastor or leader, who is an extension of God's hand for your blessing, understand that they could be blessing obstructers and feet binding grave clothes that you have to do away with, so that you don't tangle yourself out of your blessing.

The messenger might not have been what everybody possibly wished he was, but at that particular point in time he was a carrier and a transmitter of anointing and therefore an extension of God's hand. Sometimes defamation would not only obstruct an individual but a whole organisation. I remember when my Spiritual father asked me to start and lead the church branch where I still serve as senior pastor, a friend who I believe was caringly being honest with me, warned that, once I am able to gather the people and the church begins to progress, I would be pushed aside and a more experienced pastor would be imported to take over because there is a historical record of a similar incident in the organisation. As a matter of fact, it did not bother me because I did not feel capable, comfortable and qualified for the role anyway, so I could gladly do with the relief. However, that did not happen and by the grace of God I have been pastoring the same Church over a decade and God has used me as an instrument in helping to start other branches to His glory. Now to me, the whole thing has been a miracle as I know how little of God and His word I knew at the beginning!

May be as you read this book, you might be going through the same or recollecting a similar example in your life. Just remember that, God can use anyone, even those who have been described as *maniacs* to transmit and transpose you to your position and place of prominence.

The Force to comply

"You know the man and the sort of things he says," Jehu replied.

The above expression indicates that Jehu was uncomfortable to disclose the discourse between himself and the messenger of Elisha. He could not tell his companions the truth that, he had co-operated with the authority of the man they called *maniac*. If you find that you have to pretend to be on the same disrespectful and rebellious wave length with your companions in order to be accepted and for that matter you cannot feel free to be honest to them, then something is seriously wrong. It is an oppressive spirit of manipulation towards falsehood in order to keep your friendship. It is effectively a psychological bondage, from which deliverance is eminently recommended by way of detachment. Any form of peer pressure requires deliverance because not only could it end you where you do not belong but it could totally stagnate and decelerate you from your ambition in life. It can keep your feet bound but a release is yours today, in Jesus name!

The force to comply through peer pressure can even happen to the top people. Pontius Pilate is a typical example.

24 When Pilate saw that he was getting nowhere, but that instead an uproar was starting, he took water and washed his hands in front of the crowd. "I am innocent of this man's blood," he said. "It is your responsibility!"

25 All the people answered, "His blood is on us and on our children!" **26** Then he released Barabbas to them. But he had Jesus flogged, and handed him over to be crucified.   Matthew 27:24-26 NIV

Pilate caved in to political pressure. He abandoned what he knew was right. He made a decision that would please everyone while keeping himself safe. When we lay aside God's clear statements of right and wrong and make decisions based on the preferences of the crowd, we effectively compromise with lawlessness. However, God promises to honour those who do right, not those who make everyone seem right. Looking at Shadrach, Meshach and Abednego in Daniel Chapter 3, we would realize that they did what was right and God honored them by way of deliverance and promotion. May God honour too, in Jesus name!

There is a tendency for people to join a majority. Unfortunately the majority may be supporting that which is wrong. We often say 'Majority carries the vote'. Unfortunately, that is why in some cases, landslide victories in elections have turned out to be rather disappointing terms in office. It is possible for a person to speak in support of an issue merely to deceive others that he supports it, whereas he knows it is wrong. It is difficult to stand against the tide of public opinion, but it is more of evil to imply support for a matter that you secretly oppose. It's an act of mislead and if a person is pressurized into misleading others, that person has been effectively pressurized even into a curse. The Bible says,

Cursed be he that makes the blind to wander out of the way. And all the people shall say, Amen.   Deut. 27:18 KJV.

Oppressive Companions Demand Truth

12 "That's not true!" they said. "Tell us." Jehu said, "Here is what he told me: 'This is what the LORD says: I anoint you king over Israel.'"

The Companion commanders were so in control of Jehu that, they knew when he was lying and when he was being honest and for that reason, they were able to demand the truth from Jehu with an oppressive tone of voice and probably threatening gesture.

PRAYER:

- Lord, Let every door of attack on my spiritual progress be closed, in Jesus' name.
- Holy Spirit, set me on Fire for God.
- I command all my imprisoned benefits to be released in the name of Jesus!
- Lord anoint me to pull down every negative stronghold standing against me, in the name of Jesus.
- Holy Spirit anoint me with the power to pursue, overtake and recover my stolen properties from the enemy.
- Lord bring every evil counsellor and counsel against me to naught, in the name of Jesus.
- Let every blocked channel to my prosperity be opened now, in Jesus' name!

Effects of Bound Face

Lazarus was bound in the face. When your face is bound then four out of the typical five senses namely Eye (vision), ear (hearing), nose (smell) and mouth (Speech/taste) of man is technically lost, the fifth is usual hand (touch). When your face is bound it means that you cannot be identified and if you cannot be identified you cannot claim your entitlement. It does not matter the validity of your passport if you cannot be recognised you cannot be allowed port entry even though you may be entitled.

Ambiguous Identity

A bound face is an ambiguous identity and untrustworthy. Despite the fact that Lazarus had come back to life, he had no future with bound face. The implication of a spiritually bound face is that, no matter your qualification and integrity, business ventures and contracts would not be handed to you. Nobody would like to do business with someone whom he or she cannot recognise. You may be entitled to the contracts but the spiritual blindfold makes you un-recognisable as the beneficiary. There are many people that come in line for various contracts, agreements and assignments yet, they are denied. Some men have passed by and missed their delegated wives and not felt any attraction because the face of the woman has been spiritually covered. However, the God of change will command your enemies and evil wishers to lose you in Jesus name.

Mockery

A bound face puts you in danger for mockery, mistaken identity and the risk of life.

[67] Then they began to spit in Jesus' face and beat him with their fists. And some slapped him, [68] jeering, "Prophesy to us, you Messiah! Who hit you that time? Matt. 26:67-68 NLT

There is no difference between a man with a bound face and he who has spits raining into his face like Jesus had from the above scripture. He would by natural reflexes keep his eyes closed. He would not be able to identify who is slapping and who is jeering. So when Jesus

commanded that Lazarus be loosed to go, it was effectively change coming to release him from mockery into a life of honour and dignity.

Grinding in Bondage

Samson was drawn into the ungodly relations with the Philistines through his eyes which he could not restrain and unfortunately those eyes were deprived from him by being gouged out; a state representative of covered face or bound eyes.

21 But the Philistines took him, and put out his eyes, and brought him down to Gaza, and bound him with fetters of brass; and he did grind in the prison house. Judges 16:21

It is degrading to grind but even worse when it is grinding in a prison house. This is because grinding is the lowliest task for slaves. Therefore it was a reduction to the lowest ebb.

Now, considering the cause of events leading to Samson's degradation, I would recommend the strategy Job adopted in his personal, self-evaluation and decision as a way forward:

"I made a covenant with my eyes not to look lustfully at a young woman. Job 31:1

Jesus recommends another way though not literally:

And if your eye causes you to stumble, pluck it out. It is better for you to enter the kingdom of God with one eye than to have two eyes and be thrown into hell. Mark 9:47 NIV

Many a time we blame and accuse the devil for every unfortunate situation but the truth is that, he is not always solely responsible. Like this case for example, it was Samson who danced to the music of the enemy. The devil instigated and Samson co-operated. When you co-operate with the enemy it becomes a joint enterprise and you become as responsible for the consequence as the joint partner.

Disgrace

Covered face can symbolise a disgraceful state of life. So in the case of Lazarus, until he was unbound he would have been alive yet living in disgrace.

But Nahash the Ammonite replied, "I will make a treaty with you only on the condition that I gouge out the right eye of every one of you and so bring disgrace on all Israel." 1 Sam 11:2 NIV

Nahash means Serpent. Now, the serpent does not always represent the devil and deception. Christ was represented as a Bronze Serpent in Numbers 21:9. However, in this particular case, the condition offered by Nahash the serpent, was not that of healing but of destruction and therefore, a clear representation and dimension of the devil.

It's so sad that, there are a lot of people both believers and non-believer who are alive, qualified in many disciplines, good looking and of great and pleasant personalities yet living in disgrace because their faces are covered by means of spiritually gouged eyes. Some of these might have been due to treaties with a kind of 'Nahash' out of mere desperation, distress, impatience and ignorance. Nevertheless, by the shared blood of Jesus Christ, your case and situation shall be different. Your eyes shall not be gouged out, neither shall your face be covered. Your face shall be progressively transformed from glory to glory, in Jesus name!

In your distress do not look for a treaty with Nahash neither accept a pity from Him. Look up to Jesus as per Numbers 21:9 and your healing and change shall be rapid. Also remember from your earlier reading of Psalm 34:5 that, those who look to him are radiant and their faces are never covered in Shame! May your face radiate the glory of God, because your change is on the way!

No Vision

A bound face is a total restriction to vision and therefore no different from gauged out eyes. It is a state in which one has to depend on the vision and sight of others for survival but as the redemptive power of God unbounds every covering the enemy might have placed on your face or any of your love ones, I declare that you shall have and enjoy a sight and a vision of your own, in Jesus name!

I will recommend Psalm 119:18 for a prayer base: *18 Open thou mine eyes, that I may behold wondrous things out of thy law.*

When face is covered it also symbolises spiritual blindness.

17 God heard the boy crying, and the angel of God called to Hagar from heaven and said to her, "What is the matter, Hagar? Do not be afraid; God has heard the boy crying as he lies there. 18 Lift the boy up and take him by the hand, for I will make him into a great nation." 19 Then <u>God opened her eyes and she saw a well of water</u>. So she went and filled the skin with water and gave the boy a drink Gen 21:17-19 NIV.

Hagar and Ishmael were both desperate for water and could not find any. This was because Hagar, the mother's eyes were spiritually blind by her sorrow from being banished out of Abraham's house, coupled with the dying state of her only son. So even though she was close to a whole well of water, she could not see it, and because she could not see it, she could not take advantage of what God had graciously provided until God opened her eyes, spiritually.

It is very easy to be blinded by sorrow, and even render your face covered. When Mary Magdalene went to the tomb of Jesus but could not find him because He had resurrected, she was so blinded by her sorrow and tears that, even when she saw Jesus she could not recognise him. She thought he was a gardener, until Jesus spoke (John 20:15-16). A state of sorrow can be a face covering grave handkerchief or bandage. No wonder Apostle Paul says emphatically in Philippians 4:4 'rejoice in the Lord always and again I say rejoice!

It follows that, unless and until the face is uncovered and eyes spiritually functional, you can be surrounded by opportunities and yet be crying desperately just for one. I remember a song by the late Bob Marley in which he said 'in the abundance of water the fool is thirsty'. Yes, it sounds a bit harsh but that is the picture and effect a covered or bound face paints.

Hagar did not have to change locations to discover a well, her eyes only had to be opened. Her face had to be uncovered. There are many people looking for Jobs and other way outs, when God has surrounded them with ideas and opportunities in abundance. Jochebed, Moses's mother and the Israelites were believing God desperately for a deliverer, yet she had Moses and could not realise that, their deliverer was her own goodly child.

Fear is another sad effect of covered face and spiritual blindness on the part of the victim.

And Elisha prayed, "Open his eyes, LORD, so that he may see." Then the LORD opened the servant's eyes, and he looked and saw the hills full of horses and chariots of fire all around Elisha – 2 Kings 6:17 NIV

Elisha and his servant had been besieged by an Aramean army and chariots in the middle of the night. When Elisha's servant woke up, fear gripped him seeing the great multitude that had surrounded them and he exclaimed his fears to Elisha. The servant's fear got the better of him until his eyes were spiritually opened subsequent to Elisha's prayer. Isn't it sad how many people tend to see what the enemy is doing but rather blind to what God is doing and has already done? When God opened the servant's eyes, he realised that there were more horses and chariots who were for them than those of the Aramean against them. To even top it up, their Chariots were of fire but no fire was mentioned in that of the Aramean. However, this assurance and confidence did not come, until his eyes were opened and was consequently delivered from all his fears. The possible reasons why many people even Christians are bewildered with fear is because they do not see God's providence and protection in the spirit but I prophesy to you that yours shall be of a different story because your eyes are blessed in accordance with Matthew 13:16 and so shall it be in Jesus name!

A bound face is representative of a blinded mind

4 The god of this age has blinded the minds of unbelievers, so that they <u>cannot see the light</u> of the gospel that displays the glory of Christ, who is the image of God. – 2 Corinthians 4:4

The purpose of a blinded mind is to deprive the individual from benefiting from the gracious provision of God's word.

The Bible says that my people are destroyed for lack of knowledge. So by being deprived from the knowledge of God's word, destruction becomes easy and automatic. Bound face is a spiritual strategy of the enemy but change is on the way!

Open thou mine eyes, that I may behold wondrous things out of thy law – Psalm 119:18 KJV

We must pray that God will open our eyes and that of our understanding to know the hope to which he has called us, the riches of his glorious inheritance in his holy people.

Misrepresentation of Truth

A covered face can also symbolise misrepresentation of truth. It is a state of hiding and hiding is usually a consequence of guilt from past or intended sin.

It follows that no matter how alive a person may be, with a covered face he or she makes a statement of dishonesty. A statement of *'I must hide so I may not be found out'*. A statement of *'guilty by intention '*, a statement of guilty ahead of action.

In the book of Genesis for example, when God asked, 'Adam where are you?' Adam said I heard your voice in the garden and I hid myself because I was naked. Nakedness, as a mental or physical state of guilt will always induce hiding.

So even though Jesus had delivered and freed Lazarus from the captivity of Death, with a covered face, Lazarus was still under the control and restriction of the enemy to guilt ahead of action. He had to be unbound facially in order to enjoy his total freedom and salvation. There are many Christians who have been saved by the wonderful grace of God but are still being robbed of their freedom due to some form of guilt mentality.

In the story of Judah and Tamar recorded in Genesis 38, it can be realised that as Tamar covered her face she managed to deceive Judah into mistaking her for a prostitute. This caused Judah to sleep with her. An action Judah would have avoided, had Tamar's face been plain and identifiable.

Having said that, the question I ask myself is this: how did Tamar know that by pretending to be a prostitute, Judah would be unable to resist her? How did she know, that by posing as a prostitute, Judah would fall for it? Yes, Judah had lost his wife:

12 After a long time <u>Judah's wife, the daughter of Shua, died</u>. When Judah had recovered from his grief, he went up to Timnah, to the men who were shearing his sheep, and his friend Hirah the Adullamite went with him. 13 When Tamar was told, "Your father-in-law is on his way to Timnah <u>to shear his sheep</u>," - Gen 38:12 -13 NIV

Yes, losing his wife might have contributed to his desire for a woman in such circumstance. However, I cannot help but identify the lack of self-discipline with Judah and of course his inability to keep focus on goals unlike the two spies in Joshua 2:1, sent by Joshua to explore the City of Jericho. They met a prostitute called Rahab but their focus was not diverted unlike Judah. Judah had gone to Timnah with a purpose to the men who were shearing his sheep but his attention and intention became diverted.

Could it be that, Judah himself was not that straight forward after all? Could it be that, he had a weakness towards prostitutes which he had kept as a secret (covered), yet known to Tamar? I recall that Tamar used to live with Judah and his family until Judah sent her away pending the growth and marriage readiness of his third and youngest son, Shelah; a promise Judah knew very well that he would not fulfil. In other words, Judah was technically covering the face of Tamar from the truth with a false promise. Did he reap what he had sown?

Be not deceived; God is not mocked: for whatsoever a man soweth, that shall he also reap. Gal 6:7

It follows that the only people who would fall for a business and go into negotiation with a covered face person are people who are also crooks and hiding behind a cover.

More Labour Little Returns

When you engage in business of any nature with a symbolically covered face, you labour more for a proportionally less and scanty returns. It is simply a situation of exploitation.

Jacob had served Uncle Laban seven years for Rachel the woman he loved but when the time came for him to enjoy the fruit of his labour, he realised that he had been given Leah, who he did not want. This was because Leah was brought to Jacob first of all in the night when it was dark and her face traditionally covered by veil, in place of Rachel. A reward less and lower than what Jacob had worked for and in a sense, bargained for. Leah was treasurable in many ways but she was not what Jacob had laboured for and therefore despite every treasure both physical and spiritual within her, she was less than Jacob deserved.

On the other hand when your face is bound you could risk losing your dignity at a discount which is another form of exploitation. Leah ended up with a husband who did not love her. I am quite sure most women would have preferred to wait for their own turns than to allow tradition to push them into an unloving marriage. Probably at a point Leah wished her face had not been covered so Jacob could have rejected her before marital consummation.

And Leah conceived, and bare a son, and she called his name Reuben: for she said, surely the LORD hath looked upon my affliction; now therefore my <u>husband will love me</u>. Gen 29:32 KJV

From the above scripture we can safely deduce that a bound face can lead to undue and unnecessary affliction physically and even emotionally. Leah was dying to be loved.

Many are the afflictions of the righteous but the Lord delivers him out from them all –Psalm 34:19

The question we might want to ask is, how do we position ourselves for the deliverance of the Lord in times of affliction? The answer is 'Hope in God'!

Hannah was afflicted not only by her bareness but her rival Peninnah aggravated the situation with provocation. However, by trusting in the God who is the giver of Children, her deliverance came. It takes, active faith, tenacity in prayer and trusting the God of change who makes all things beautiful in His own time, to see your deliverance.

When Hannah's deliverance came, she knew the source and so did Leah when her son came. May you know the source of your deliverance when your change comes!

Nose – No Smell

With Lazarus's face covered his ability to smell was hindered by virtue of his most probably covered nose. So though he had been called back to life he could not smell adequately. The ability to smell adequately has a decisive and conclusive power. Hence the adage, 'wake *up and smell the coffee'*. In other words, get serious and face reality.

In the story of Isaac preparing to bless Jacob, he only became convinced of Jacob's identity to be Esau, when he had smelled his cloak.

And he came near, and kissed him: and he smelled the smell of his clothing, and blessed him, and said, See, the smell of my son is as the smell of a field which the LORD has blessed: Gen 27:27 KJV

It was due to the smell of the field that Isaac caught in Jacob's cloak that made him conclude that he was blessing the right person. It was a decisive moment and move because prior to that point, Isaac had exhausted almost all his available senses. He had touched and heard

Jacob. For he had said, the voice is Jacob's but the hand is Esau's. He had tasted the venison to validate the standard recipe. The only thing left was the conclusive smell of the field on a hunter.

I remember I had a problem with my sinuses when I was younger. I could not smell too well. One day my dad came home from work and smelt gas as he entered the house. Our gas was leaking. How long for, I had no idea. However, living in Ghana a hot country, we usually kept the windows opened and the outer doors sieved up, in order for fresh air to circulate well. My Dad took me to the doctors, I had x-rays and various tests done but had no proper diagnosis so the problem persisted with all the associated risks. One day, I decided to pray for my healing. I don't know when I became healed, but all I can say is that, now I smell from afar and able to locate exact source even though not to the extent of trained dogs and I appreciate God for a remarkable healing and the effective change he has brought to me.

The ability to smell is needed to overcome risks such as gas leakages, among others that could pose a defeat to the object of calling back to life, he who was dead.

Ears – Testimonies

The Bible says that faith cometh by hearing and hearing comes by the word of God. It means that with the face/ head bound, hearing was restricted. In 2 Kings 18, Elijah needed to hear the encouraging instruction of God in order to follow directions to Zarephath whiles in Genesis 26, Isaac needed to hear the discouraging instruction of God from going down to Egypt but to stay in Gera for His blessing.

In the Story of the woman with the issue of blood in Mark 5, her faith began with the testimonies she had heard about Jesus. Furthermore, the fact that Jesus was in town motivated and inspired her beyond her weak and resistant health to press on towards touching the hem of the Lord's garment for her healing! She was weak but her ability to hear was what commenced her change.

Likewise the story of the nobleman in John 4; the nobleman travelled that long distance to solicit the healing of Jesus for his son due to the facts he heard about Jesus. When hearing is spiritually interfered with, you are deprived from living testimonies that ignite your miracles, but I prophesy to you according to Matthew 13:16 that, your ears are blessed and therefore you will hear and hear good news; good news that would inspire and take you to an expected end, in Jesus name!

The Mouth and Tongue

When the face is bound round about, the mouth is automatically covered and when the mouth is covered the tongue becomes almost useless. Not only is taste therefore impossible but confession and declaration are restricted. However, Bible says 'with the mouth confession is made unto righteousness' (Rom 10:10). It is quite probable that many who have not been born again are face bound, therefore not only can they not hear the gospel, they cannot confess with their mouth because, spiritually they might be bound. Furthermore, the Bible says, if you have faith like a mustard seed you will 'say '...and it will be so. With the mouth and assistance of the tongue, we utter words by faith to bind and to loose. We utter words to enforce the will of God upon the earth. In 1 Kings 17, as an example, Elijah was able to stop the rains and dew from falling and by the same mouth, he was able to reverse the condition. It means that, when the mouth is spiritually covered you cannot engage in the spiritual battle of words.

I am the LORD thy God, which brought thee out of the land of Egypt: open thy mouth wide, and I will fill it. Psalm 81:10 KJV

You need the ability and freedom of opening your mouth and praying to God because for sure, He has a trail of acts for which you already have testimonies, just like the Israelites, in and out from Egypt. If you can confidently trust and depend on him by opening your mouth widely and boldly in petition like a baby at his mother's breasts, he will fill it with the bountiful strength of praise that silences the enemy and avenger. Bible says 'Because of Your adversaries, you have established a stronghold from the mouths of children and nursing infants to silence the enemy and the avenger'. Psalm 8:2 HCSB

Note that, nursing infants are totally dependent on their mothers and that is how it should be for us, as children of God. Amen!

In Joshua chapter 6, the Israelites proved their trust in God at the Walls of Jericho. However, they needed their mouths in order to give the loud shout of praise that stimulated the supernatural power of God to bring down the walls of Jericho. So a mouth of praise stimulates the supernatural power of God into a victorious action for us.

Hence, we can deduce that when the mouth is covered, ability to praise is affected. May your face be unbound to release the mandated, effective and powerful use of your mouth in Jesus name!

O Lord, open thou my lips; and my mouth shall shew forth thy praise. Psalm 51:15 KJV

CHAPTER 15

CONCLUSION

God is good, God is loving and always ready to meet the needs of man. However, He does not physically come down but uses instruments he has already prepared as agents. He uses instruments usually within a good proximity of the needy areas or persons. A lot of times God uses people but the onus is on the beneficiary to identify the instrument God has prepared for his or her change, in other not to expel rather than embrace him. So in the story about the Shunamite woman in 1 kings 6 for example, Elisha was God's instrument and agent for the change the woman had probably hoped for all her marital years. The good thing is that, she did not miss Elisha. Although God is the God of second chances, no one knows when the second chance would appear or arrive. Therefore if the first chance was taken for granted and missed, the risk of unpreparedness could fail the surprise of the second chance as well.

It is important to appreciate that, once the need for change has been communicated to God through prayer, the answer has been dispatched and could be in any packaging especially in human form. It is also important as a person to keep in mind that, you are an instrument of God on earth to facilitate desirable changes in the lives of the needy and for that reason, God is always ready to use you. However, you must also ensure that, you are always ready to be used too.

Elisha did not miss his purpose as a change agent neither did the Shunamite woman miss her opportunity, I trust that you will neither miss yours in either way. Amen.

Whenever you identify your change agents or companions, be ready to co-operate with them but more importantly co-operate with God, through His word. The Bible says, if you give to a prophet in the name of a prophet, you would receive a prophet's reward. By the Shunamite co-operating with the word of God, she did not miss her change. As a matter of fact, she was blessed with a life in the form of a son, whereas the same Elisha was met by some young boys who decided to make fun of him (2Kings 2:23-24 NLT) ended up losing their lives through a curse. Remember that the Bible says, a curse without a cause will not stand (Proverbs 26:2). So if the Curse stood, it confirms that, there was a valid cause. The disciples had to co-operate with Jesus to change them from fishermen to fishers of men. Likewise, you must co-operate with your change agents as well as your change gifts from God.

Faithfulness and commitment to duty always pays. Wherever and in whatever situation you find yourself, be poised to exhibit faithfulness just as our Lord Jesus Christ was faithfully committed to his duty here on earth and that faithfulness will attract unprecedented rewards to you. Amen.

I remember in the book of Esther, even though God's name was not mentioned once throughout the book, evidence of His providence was projected all through. From the disposition of Queen Vashti to the promotion of Esther, it was all about faithfulness! Now, even though the book focuses on Esther and was named after her accordingly, I cannot help but applaud the underlying faithfulness of Mordecai, Esther's cousin not only as an agent of change but for the undeniable effect of faithfulness, no matter what. Mordecai was a gatekeeper in the Palace and he performed this task with commitment and with so much dedication that even though he was a slave in exile, he was always stationed accordingly. Now interestingly, when Bigthana and Teresh wanted to conspire against the King, they lost thought of their surroundings to the extent that they planned within the hearing reach of Mordecai, who was minding the gate faithfully. Now, had Mordecai moved or diminished in his commitment at the gate, he could have missed the vital information he needed to serve and protect the King and that would have changed the whole story about the Israelites. It is very possible that somebody's life change hangs on your faithfulness to the King of kings. The subject of being a faithful messenger would always end in refreshment. Change is on the way and you will not miss it as a faithful servant and messenger.

Whatever change you desire and are expecting must be met with prepared accommodation. Preparation is a vital element in embracing the change that God is bringing your way. You must get ready to accommodate the answers God is bringing to your prayers for a change in your circumstances no matter, how small or how big and no matter what it is. As the saying goes, failing to prepare is preparing to fail. Remember the five foolish virgins? Be prepared!

Before the Israelites crossed the Jordan, Joshua told the Israelites to consecrate themselves for the next day, the Lord was going to do wonders. The need for preparation is vital in seeing and embracing your change.

Testifying and giving thanks is a good way to prepare for extra change. My presiding Bishop, often says, 'your gratitude will determine your altitude'. In other words, the more grateful you are and express to God, the more He ensures that He elevates you. As we saw earlier regarding the ten lepers, it was the gratitude of the one out of the ten that brought about the increase in his change. Of a similar pattern in Malachi 3:10, the unchanging God promises us of abundant incremental change, as we honour him with the tithe (one in ten) of our increase.

Availability is a key, so do your best to be available for the things of God. The stone water Jars were available when needed. God will always work with what we avail, in order to bring the desired change in our lives and circumstances. In the story of the feeding of five thousand for example, Jesus used the five loaves and two fishes that were availed, to bring about the miraculous feeding. Interestingly, the focus and message of the left overs was not so much on the fishes but rather the bread which were few, but five in number (Mark 8:19). The number five is symbolic of grace. I believe the bread turning out to be more than enough is a reminder that, the grace of God is always sufficient no matter the increase and enormity of our needs!

Likewise, in the story of the widow whose husband the prophet, left her a huge debt and was faced with the threat of losing her sons as bondsmen to the debt collectors; upon consultation with Prophet Elisha, Elisha asked her for what she had in her house. In other words, her desired change was dependent on what she was willing to avail. Availability is what makes the difference not ability. God works with potential, not potency. That is one of the reasons why he would pick Gideon from the smallest tribe and least clan to fight victoriously for all the clans and tribes of Israel. He had chosen Gideon by availability not qualification. The widow's oil which she described as 'nothing but little' was just like Gideon. Least in all aspects but the availability brought the desired change. Your change is also on the way, but your availability would certainly facilitate your testimony.

The effectual fervent prayer of the righteous availeth much. Never rule out the tool and potency of prayer because prayer offered by faith works. Your prayer ignites and sparks change firstly in the spiritual realms and then manifests physically. Many changes have occurred through the initiation of prayer. Plans and plots of the enemy have been averted for the benefit of God's people through Prayer. Peter was imprisoned by Herod but he miraculously escaped from the prison due to a corporate prayer offered in the priesthood home of Mary. Those prayers sent forth a change to the prison. It shattered every security system of Herod's prison! Other situations like that of Jonah had been changed through the employment of Prayer, such that he escaped from the mouth of the big fish (Jonah 2). God will hear your prayer for change no matter where you offer it. Whether at a priesthood home or in the belly of a fish. If you can pray, just pray and see God command a release to His glory.

If you can manage, ensure that you surround yourself with good friends. A good friend is not the one who would necessarily tell you what you want to hear always. They will tell you the truth and it is the truth that makes us free. The Bible says 'Wounds from a sincere friend are better than many kisses from an enemy' (Proverbs 27:6 NLT). From what we have learnt about counsel and with the further assistance of the Holy Spirit, I pray that you would be able to identify good friends based on their counsel. Endeavour to walk in the counsel of the Godly even if it deprives you of your preferred desire. A good counsel would be in line with the word of God so as often as you can, relate the counsel you receive to the word of God. The Bible says in 1 Corinthians 15:33 NIV 'Do not be misled: Bad company corrupts good character.' Do not allow wrong company to swallow and manipulate you away from the change God is bringing your way like what nearly obstructed Jehu, in what we looked at earlier.

No matter how long your desired change takes, wait for it because delays are not denials from God. Bible encourages that, the vision is for an appointed time and at the end, it will speak. Though it tarries, wait for it for it will surely come to pass, it will not tarry. Be encouraged that, a thousand years is not for ever, neither will it outlive God's words and promises.

I must say that the act of waiting is not about idleness but a process of inter weaving your strength with that of God's, depending and spending time in presence. The process of waiting is also about serving God in every capacity and with humility and honour just as waiters in a restaurant do to their precious customers.

No matter your circumstances and the length of time lapse, expect what God has said to manifest. May be it's a situation of marital delay. If you are meant to marry, then your wife or husband is definitely out there. It's a matter of availability and positioning. May be it's a matter of delayed child bearing. Remember that it's never too late with God. However, do not neglect the role of prayer. Isaac married Rebecca at the age of forty years but did not see their first child till Isaac was sixty years old. This happened after Isaac had prayed on behalf of Rebecca. They were blessed with twins. Esau and Jacob. May be you have been married for a number of years and getting worried. No matter the situation, it's never too late. It cannot be any worse than the situation of Lazarus in which we saw God ruling over time and decay. Your change is on the way because God is interested in seeing your breakthrough and not your breakdown. He is interested in His glory shining through your circumstance and to give you double for your trouble like Isaac and Rebecca.

When your change comes some would not be able to recognise you. Your testimony could even spark admirable arguments and you might be needed to settle and testify to the glory of God.

8 His neighbours and those who had formerly seen him begging asked, "Isn't this the same man who used to sit and beg?" 9 Some claimed that he was. Others said, "No, he only looks like him." But he himself insisted, "I am the man." - John 9:8-9 NIV

Yes, many will be amazed at what God is about to do with you. Your future shall bear no resemblance to your past.

I remember when I went to university as a matured student. I was already a father of three boys. I took a degree course in Information Systems. At that time I had not turned on a computer before. I was so fresh and ill-informed that, I failed our first practical test. It was too basic a test for a degree pursuing student to fail. My name and another consolatory classmate were posted on the notice board indicating our failure and need to redo the test. I asked a fellow student who was more experienced, to teach me in preparation for the test and that was where I exposed my intolerable ignorance to the extent that, my helper got frustrated and gave up on me. I tried and solicited help from another young gentleman who happened to come from the same country as me. He was about twelve years younger than me. It was quite embarrassing but I managed it and also managed to pass the re-sit, though just on the border line. By this time I guess I had been given a nickname in the year group and also written off. However, I started working harder though very difficult considering how little I knew, the family commitments I had to fulfil as a father, husband, student and a part-time worker in the UK. By the grace of God, I managed to scrape through the subsequent exams with a few referrals here and there.

I did a sandwich course of four years, so I spent the third year in the industry working for one of the top sugar refinery companies in the UK. They managed to keep patient with my slow pace. However, by the end of the placement my knowledge and confidence had rocketed high. I had learnt new things and technologies very few of my colleagues had heard about, in addition to what we had all been taught. I began finishing assignments quicker and my contributions at lectures were to industrial standards and best practise. Some students began to ask for my assistance in our assignments,
whiles others wanted to have me in their groups for group works. Unfortunately for those who made fun of me, even when they struggled in their work they could not ask for my assistance, though I could be sitting right next to them. I had become like 'the carpenter's son'. You would not think I have ever had to re-sit a test. Praise God! The change was radical and remarkable. I graduated with a good degree and was blessed with a good job in which God granted me success to the level of Senior Consultant.

God is certainly going to bring change your way too, but humility, availability and a teachable spirit would help. Don't be ashamed to declare your ignorance because even the most knowledgeable person was once ignorant of something. Ask for help where and when you need it and you will not miss your change and chance.

Change is on the way, bringing an end to begging like it did in the life of the boy born blind. So get ready for an introduction to boasting in the God of change because you are about to lend to many, without borrowing from any.

Keep trusting God, do your responsible part as a faithful servant of God and God himself would do the rest as the faithful master. Remember when obedience marries God's instruction, a miracle is born. Get ready for your miracle, get ready for your testimony because change is on the way and you will not miss it.

To God Be All Glory and Honour.